Export Import Practices: ASEAN Focus

Hla Theingi

Export Import Practices: ASEAN Focus, **1st edition**

Author:
Hla Theingi

Language editor:
Bharthi Limbuni

ISBN-13: 978-1484994047

ISBN-10: 1484994043

Preface

This book is designed preliminary for students taking international business management as their major or minor. The book emphasizes on export import environments and practices in ASEAN countries. Students will be familiar with the complexity and the formalities of international trade transactions.

The book comprises of 12 chapters emphasizing on the issues involved in developing comprehensive export/import strategies at firm levels. Topics include the strategic use of export/import instruments/packages offered by organizations to achieve economic and competitive advantages; procedures and practices of export-import transactions, export-import compliance, documentation, financing, export-import channels and transportation modes.

It should be noted that this book does not cover every detail in each domain; further study is recommended.

However, I hope this book would serve as a useful tool to assist the students to comprehend the basic philosophy of export and import strategies and finally put into practice in running the export import business.

Acknowledgements

It is a rare pleasure for me to express my profound gratitude and many thanks to the following individuals.

I am greatly indebted to the authors whose names are cited in the references and throughout this book.

My heartfelt thanks to my husband, and my daughter and sons who have understood me and encouraged me throughout the production of this book and are the sources of my spirit and strength, helping me to overcome all the difficulties and challenges in writing this book.

I also extend my appreciation to Dr. Cherdpong Sibunruang, the Dean of Martin De Tour School of Management and Economics, Dr. Radha Sirinukul, the Chairperson of International Business Management Department, assistant professor Dr. Theingi, and Dr. Suppanuntra Rompraset for their cooperation and encouragement, Ms. Bharthi Limbuni for her editing work and Mr. Khin Maung Lwin for the valuable photos.

I must say that without any of them it would not have been possible for me to complete this book.

Table of Contents

List of Abbreviations

AEC	: ASEAN Economic Community
AFTA	: ASEAN Free Trade Area
AR	: All Risks
ASEAN	: Association of South East Asian Nations
ATA	: Admission Temporary Admission
B/C	: Bill for collection
B/E	: Bill of Exchange
B/L	: Bill of lading
BDV	: Brussels Definition of Value
BOI	: Board of Investment
BRICS	: Brazil, Russia, India, China, South Africa
CEPT	: Common Effective Preferential Tariff
CFR	: Cost and Freight
CFS	: Container Freight Station
CIF	: Cost Insurance and Freight
CIP	: Carriage and Insurance Paid to
CISG	: Convention on the International Sales of Goods
CoA	: Certificate of Analysis
CRM	: Certified Reference Material

CY	: Container Yard
D/A	: Document against Acceptance
D/P	: Document against Payment
DAP	: Delivered At Place
DAT	: Delivered At Terminal
DDP	: Delivered Duty Paid
EDI	: Electronic Data Exchange
EMC	: Export Management Company
EPZ	: Export Processing Zone
EU	: European Union
EXIM	: Export-Import
EXW	: Ex Work
FAO	: Food and Agriculture Organization
FAS	: Free Alongside Ship
FCA	: Free Carrier
FCL	: Full Container Load
FDI	: Foreign Direct Investment
FI	: Free In
FIO	: Free In Out
FO	: Free Out
FOB	: Free on Board

FPA	: Free of particular Average
FTA	: Free Trade Area
FTZ	: Free Trade Zone
GATT	: General Agreement on Trade and Tariffs
GSP	: Generalized System of Preference
GST	: Goods & Service Tax
GTV	: GATT Transaction Value
HAWA	: House Air Waybill
HS	: Harmonized System
ICC	: International Chamber of Commerce
ICD	: Inland Container Deport
IEAT	: Industrial Estate Authority of Thailand
IMF	: International Monetary Fund
Incoterms	: International Commercial Terms
LC	: Letter of Credit
LCL	: Less than Container Load
LO/LO	: Lift On/Lift Off
LOI	: Letter of Indemnity
MAWB	: Master Air Waybill
MERCOSUR	: Southern Cone Common Market
NAFTA	: North American Free Trade Area

NTB	: Non Tariff Barriers
NVO	: Non-Vessel Owner
NVOCC	: Non-Vessel-Operating Common Carrier
PO	: Purchase Order
PPQ	: Plant Protection and Quarantine
R&D	: Research and Development
RO RO	: Roll On/ Roll Off
SCR	: Special Commodity Rates
SCT	: Special Consumption Tax
SEZs	: Special Economic Zones
T/T	: Telegraphic Transfer
TEU	: Twenty-feet Equivalent Units
TIR	: Transport International Routier
UCP	: Uniform Custom Practice
UNCTAD	: United Nations Convention of Trade and Development
VAT	: Value Added Tax
WTO	: World Trade Organization

1 Introduction to Export Import Management

International Trade Theories such as the absolute advantage theory by Adam Smith, the comparative advantage theory by David Ricardo, the factor proportion theory by E. Heckeher & B. Ohlin, the product life cycle theory by Raymond Vernon, and the national competitive advantage theory by Micahel E. Poter have evolved over time. These trade theories explore why nations trade with one another, the benefits and patterns of international trade.

The benefits derived from international trade[1] include cheaper goods, greater product variety, economies of scale, job creation, technology transfer and ultimately raising standard of living. Though there are a lot of benefits derived from international trade, there are also some arguments against international trade. These arguments are based on environmental deterioration, domestic job losses, workers' exploitation, extinction of culture and national sovereignty.

Globalization and International Trade

The world is moving away from self-contained national economies towards an interdependent, integrated global economic system. Globalization has taken place all over the world. The business world is changing faster and is becoming more unpredictable than ever. Advances in telecommunication, transport and production process have increased the speed of globalization. Advances in telecommunications enable speedier and more effective communication within and between firms. Advances in transports facilitate speedier and more efficient movement of

---

[1] International trade means selling and buying goods and services across national boundaries called export and import. Export includes all activities that transfer products and services from domestic producers to consumers in foreign countries. Import includes all activities that transfer products and services from foreign producers to consumers in home country.

goods and people within and between countries, and advances in production processes such as flexible production systems facilitate cost-effective production strategies and global outsourcing. Along with these advances, converging tastes and preferences of consumers and falling trade barriers through the formation of bilateral and multilateral trade agreements such as North American Free Trade Area (NAFA), Asian Free Trade Area (AFTA) make it easier for firms to trade internationally.

The gravity of economic activity is shifting towards Asia. Businesses in Asia have low debt-to-equity ratio and the region's private and household savings rate is high at an average of more than 30 percent as compared to savings in the United States which is at 4 percent of the national income. Higher savings rates in Asia would help Asian economies grow from within through consumption and investment (Seetalavajit, 2010). Thus economists expect that Asia will likely dominate the global economy and capture more than half of the world's gross domestic product (GDP) by 2030 (Seetalavajit, 2010). As of 2010, Asia's economic share is 37 percent of the world's GDP.

Markets are expanding worldwide, which create interdependencies of economies, workforce mobility, global production and outsourcing. The emergence of a dynamic South[2] as an additional (to the North) engine for world trade and new investment, and an expansion in South-South trade in goods, services and commodities are examples in this regard.

Thus, to stay competitive, businesses need to move along with the changes and achieve the speed, flexibility and resilience to handle the economic and market changes on a worldwide basis. Bernd Waltermann, senior partner and managing director of BCG (Singapore), in his presentation on

---

[2] Trading among developing countries for example, ASEAN intra regional trade has been increased, instead of US, EU being developing countries' ' major export markets.

competitiveness at the Thailand Management Association's seminar has put forth the following questions for companies to consider (Deboonme, 2010):

- What is the advantage of expansion? Can we expand further?
- Can international exposure increase competitiveness? Which areas?
- Which business model to pursue?
- Which countries should be prioritized?
- What level of resources (capital, people) is needed to expand internationally? How can they be mobilized?
- What are the potential risks and rewards?

The answers to these questions will enable companies to maintain competitiveness in the global arena.

Along with the globalization, international institutions such as the World Trade Organization (WTO), the International Monetary Fund (IMF), and the World Bank, have evolved over the past half century. They are needed to help manage, regulate, and police the global marketplace and promote the establishment of multinational treaties to govern the global business system.

Export and Import Management

Export and import management is a part of international business management that deals with the professional handling of activities in international trade from negotiating trade deals to expediting transactions. Export import management is a great concern for export-manufacturers, export-traders, service exporters such as banks, insurance companies, transportation companies, freight forwarders, and importers. New exporters and importers encounter several problems such as failure to obtain qualified export counseling in developing an export plan, underestimating the complexity and cost of overseas transportation (shipping) and custom clearance, unwillingness to modify products to meet other countries' regulations or cultural preferences.

Designing a proper export – import plan and strategies is important and helps managers avoid or reduce problems and risks which they might encounter in international business transaction chains. An international transaction chain consists of all activities involved in export of goods or services, such as export/ import financing, credit check of the trading partners, transportation, custom clearance, etc. A successful strategy must evaluate the elements of the transaction chain. Thorough understanding of each element of the international transaction chain, managers can develop efficient export import policies and strategies. The following Figure 1 shows the elements of international business transaction chain. In the following chapters each element of international business transaction chain are discussed in details.

This book is divided into twelve chapters as follows:

Chapter 1 is the introduction to export import management, presenting globalization and international trade together with the significance of proper export import strategies formation and planning.

Chapter 2 discusses the export import environment and market selection procedure. Accessing the company's core competencies is the main concern of the firm. The firm's external environment such as political, legal, social, economic, infrastructure and technological environment together with significance of industry level analysis are discussed. Moreover, practical insights with more emphasis on ASEAN countries as examples are presented.

Chapter 3 describes export import promotions and privileges. In order to achieve the economic goal of many countries, the countries' governments offer different packages of trade promotions and privileges. Export-Import promotions and

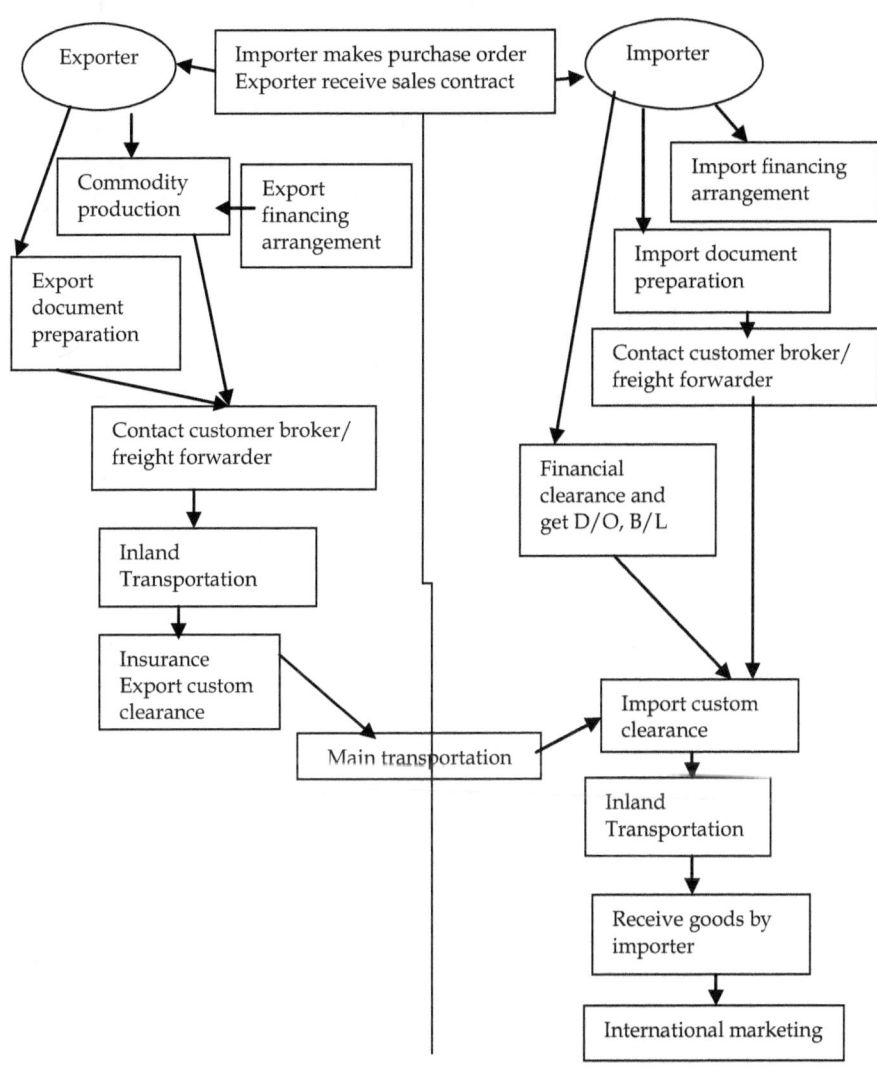

Activities in country of origin   Activities in country of destination

Figure: 1 International Business Transaction Chain

privileges provided by the Kingdom of Thailand are discussed in detail. In addition, some of the promotional packages provided by the Lao People's Democratic Republic, the Kingdom of Cambodia, the Republic of the Union of Myanmar and the Republic of Singapore are presented.

Chapter 4 presents customs formalities for export and import and particularly tariff classification, custom valuation and customs procedures are discussed. Tariff structure in ASEAN countries is discussed in detail.

Chapter 5 discusses the International Commercial TERMS (INCOTERMS). In order to eliminate uncertainties and different interpretations of trade terms on a world wide scale due to distance, language and local business practices differences, the International Chamber of Commerce (ICC) developed and published INCOTERMS. The latest INCOTERMS 2010 are discussed in detail.

Chapter 6 presents documents needed to be prepared by exporters and importers. The purpose of each document is discussed in detail.

Chapter 7 discusses terms of payments used by exporters and importers. Concern about mistrust across international borders is natural. Method of payment may

Chapter 8 explains export import financing sources. It also explains the banks' role and their services in facilitating international trade.

Chapter 9 presents global transportation. Since products are rarely produced and consumed in the same location, movement of goods from one place to another requires proper transportation platform. Road, rail, ocean, air and pipe line transportation modes are discussed in detail.

Chapter 10 presents export import insurance. All experienced traders are aware of the risks of their cargos while they are in transit. Hence, export import cargo insurance and export import credit insurance are explained.

Chapter 11 briefly introduces the elements of international marketing mix.

Finally, Chapter 12 concludes the overall export and import strategies and practices. This chapter also presents the cost structure starting from the exporter's warehouse to the importer's warehouse. After studying the text, students are to develop their own strategies and put them into practice in running the export import business.

References
- Deboonme, A. (2010). The challenges of expanding successfully in foreign arena. *The Nation*.
- Seetalavajit, S. (2010, 1.12.2010). Asia tipped for global economic dominance *The Nation*.

2   Export Import Environment

Selecting overseas markets is critical for many firms. With increasing dependence on global markets for sustainable growth, the relevance of situational analysis and of decision making becomes more and more important.

Prior to the selection of the target market, firms need to evaluate their competitive position in terms of the key success factors such as capabilities, resources and skills needed to succeed in the oversea market.

Internal Environmental Analysis

Accessing the company's core competencies is the main concern of the firm. Understanding a firm's strengths and weaknesses help the firm formulates its competitive strategy. The firm's internal analysis mainly includes analyses of the firm's financial resources, management resources and technology resources. By analyzing its own strengths and weaknesses in the following areas; business objectives and strategies, possession of resources and skills, strength of asset and competitiveness, relative brand strength, distribution strength, customer loyalty, strategic flexibility, access to information, experience in host country, etc, management can select strategies consistent with the firm's particular strengths and the market conditions it faces. An executive decision is made on which foreign market to enter, the timing and the most desirable entry mode based on the firm's assessment of its own propensity to take risks and the expected level of achievement of the goals the firm has set in the foreign market (Phatak, 2009).

In addition to knowledge of own strengths and weaknesses, it is also imperative to understand the external environment of the firm. Thus, firm need to do country level analysis and industry level analysis.

External Environmental Analysis

To be a successful international market expansion, it is very important to have a fit between what the firm wants to offer in the market and what the consumers in the market want.

The whole world markets can be firm's prospective markets. The question is whether a firm should go to all of the markets simultaneously or a firm should prioritize the market. The international business literature proposes a systematic approach to international market expansion. The international market expansion process is composed of three stages (Demirbag, 2010; Koch, 2001; Kumar, 1994; Sakarya, 2007; Wood, 2000). First, firms need to do preliminary screening of markets. Individual markets are roughly reviewed by considering the basic fit between customer preferences and the firm's existing product line, and then study the market size, market growth rate, competitive intensity and rivalry, political stability, geographical distance, economic development and so on. Then firms will eliminate the unfeasible markets. This will help firms to reduce time and effort regarding detail analysis of every market. At the end of the first preliminary screening of markets, the firm will have a handful of markets which have the most potential.

In the second stage, in-depth screening of those handfuls of markets is to be carried out. In depth screening includes detailed analyses of each country's external environment information called Political and Legal, Economic, Socio - cultural and Technology and Infrastructure (PEST) analysis (country level analysis) and competitor analyses (industry analysis). Market potential estimation, market growth rate forecast, strength and weaknesses of competition, entry barriers are revisited to obtain information about the different business environments, cultural disparities and market conditions. The detail analyses of firm's external export import environments are discussed in the following section.

Finally, firms will select the optimal market. The final selection is carried out by finding country markets which best leverages the firms' available resources together with financial net present value analysis.

Political and Legal Environment

Political and legal attributes such as level of political stability, protection of private property, attitude towards foreign products and foreign direct investment (FDI), trade and investment restrictions and promotions, red tapes and corruptions, ease of operations, regulatory environment such as protection of intellectual property rights, local laws regarding marketing and advertising, production, environmental standards and the like influence the firm's strategy and management.

One prominent example is Google in China. China renewed Google's license to operate in the country only after Google agreed to respect the Chinese censorship law. Google had to agree that "it will not provide any information that will endanger China's national security, damage China's national interests, instigate ethnic hatred, spread superstitious information, damage social stability, or (provide) pornography, violence or slanderous information" (Agence France-Press, 2010).

Different countries use different political systems from totalitarianism (communism, socialism) at one extreme to pluralism and anarchism (Democracy) at the other extreme. Different legal systems are used in different countries as well. Countries can apply common laws[3], civil laws[4] or/and theocratic laws[5]. Nevertheless, stable political environment with strong legal framework favors doing business in such a country.

Trade Agreements

Trade policies of countries vary from preventive to laissez-faire policies. Types of trade restrictions and trade promotions are also of concern to the trading firms. Due to memberships in

---

[3] Common Law is based on tradition, precedent, and usage. The following countries practice common law; US, Canada, Australia, New Zealand, Nigeria.
[4] Civil Law is based on detailed set of laws organized into codes. France, Germany, Japan, Thailand and much of South America, practice civil law.
[5] Theocratic Law is based on religious teachings (Islamic law).

international organizations such as WTO, bilateral and multilateral trade agreements among countries and economic integrations, many countries' trade policies have become less restrictive.

One of the prominent multilateral trade agreements; **ASEAN Free Trade Area (AFTA) agreement** was made among Southeast Asian nations. The Association of Southeast Asian Nations (ASEAN) was established in 1967. It has become one of the world's most successful regional economic integrations. ASEAN currently consists of ten members namely, Brunei, Cambodia, Indonesia, Laos, Myanmar, the Philippines, Singapore, Thailand and Vietnam.

AFTA agreement was signed in 1992 in Singapore. The primary goals of AFTA are to increase ASEAN's competitive edge as a production base in the world market through the elimination of tariff and non-tariff barriers within ASEAN and to attract more foreign direct investment to ASEAN.

The primary mechanism to achieve the goal is the Common Effective Preferential Tariff (CEPT) scheme with gradual tariff reductions. The CEPT only applies to goods originating within ASEAN. The general rule is that local ASEAN content must be at least 40% of the Free on Board (FOB) value of the goods. The local ASEAN content can be cumulative, that is, the value of inputs from various ASEAN members can be combined to meet the 40% requirement. The exporter must obtain a "Form D" certification from its national government attesting that the goods have met the 40% requirement. The Form D must be presented to the customs authority of the importing government to qualify for the CEPT rate.

At the 2003 ASEAN summit in Bali, Indonesia, ASEAN leaders agreed to integrate their economies by 2020 and establish ASEAN Economic Community (AEC). At the 2007 ASEAN summit in Cebu, Philippines, the dead line to realize the AEC was brought forward by five years to 2015. The goals of AEC are as follows (The ASEAN Secretariat, 2008):

o to be single market and production base

    o where the initial ASEAN member (ASEAN 6) countries have reduced import duties on most goods (exclusive of products in sensitive and highly sensitive list) to zero percent since 1 January 2010. ASEAN's newer members, namely Cambodia, Laos, Myanmar and Vietnam (CLMV countries) are to reduce import duty to zero percent by 1 January 2015.

o where there will be significant reduction on restrictions to ASEAN service suppliers in providing services and in establishing companies across national borders within the region. ASEAN members are committed to increase foreign equity participation to at least 70% in the service sectors. As an initial step service sectors such as Information and Communication Technology, Health, Tourism, Air Transport, and Logistic sector will be liberalized by 2013 and the rest by 2015.

o where ASEAN Investment Co-operation is implemented through the ASEAN Investment Area (AIA) which was signed in 1998. Under the AIA, all industries (manufacturing, agriculture, fishery, forestry and mining and services) incidental to these five sectors are to be opened and national treatment granted to investors. Members are to extend nondiscriminatory treatment to investors within the ASEAN. In 2009 AIA was revised and the amended agreement ASEAN Comprehensive Investment Agreement (ACIA) was signed in order to further accelerate investments among members. ACIA is a comprehensive agreement covering liberalization, protection, facilitation and promotion of investments.

o where freer flow of capital is to be allowed by removing or relaxing restrictions on capital flows and supporting foreign direct investment and initiatives to promote capital market developments.

o where member countries will allow mobility of natural persons engaged in trade, goods and services and investments by facilitating the issuance of visas and employment passes for ASEAN professionals and skilled labor. In facilitating the free flow of services provided by those natural persons (by 2015), ASEAN is also working towards harmonization and standardization through Mutually Recognizatioin Agreements (MRAs). MRA enables the qualifications of service suppliers recognized by one ASEAN country to be mutually recognized by other ASEAN members. Currently 7 MRAs have been concluded for the following professionals; engineers, medical practitioners, nurses, dentists, land surveyors, accountants and architects.

- AEC aims to enhance cooperation among ASEAN University Network (AUN) members to increase mobility for both students and staff within the region; to develop core competencies and qualifications for job/occupational and trainers skills required in the priority services sectors (by 2009); and in other services sectors (from 2010 to 2015); and to strengthen the research capabilities of each ASEAN member country in terms of promoting skills, job placements, and developing labor market information networks among ASEAN member countries.

o to be a competitive economic region
  o by enhancing e-ASEAN, taxation, competition policy, intellectual property, consumer protection and infrastructural development
o to have equitable economic development by
  o narrowing development gap between ASEAN-6 and CLMV and
  o supporting development of SMEs.
o and to integrate into the global economy by
  o having coherent approach toward external economic relations
  o enhanced participation in global supply network and

o having free trade agreements with non-ASEAN countries

Once AEC is fully implemented in 2015, it will transform ASEAN into a region with freer flow of goods, services, investments, skilled labor and freer flow of capital. As a result by 2015, ASEAN will become mega-economy of the world with a population of 600 million and GDP of more than US$2.5 trillion. Besides, ASEAN has multilateral trade agreements with many countries such as China, Japan, Korea (called ASEAN + 3), together with Australia, New Zealand and India (called ASEAN + 6). ASEAN + 6 will have total population of 3,268 million which is about 50% of global population with 22% of global GDP (Saquandeekul, 2010).

European Union (EU) is interested in having bilateral trade agreement with ASEAN, however, EU is more interested to use piecemeal approach to trading with countries in ASEAN. EU has started bilateral negotiations with Asean members Singapore, Malaysia and Vietnam. Indonesia and the Philippines are also preparing for negotiations, while Thailand has not yet submitted its official agreement. Thailand has agreed to set up 14 subcommittees to consider various issues in talks for Thailand EU FTA. Practical insight 2.1 presents EU's aspiration to have piecemeal approach to trading with countries in ASEAN.

AEC will liberalize, facilitate, and promote the investment in the region to ASEAN investors and ASEAN – based foreign investors. Thus, ASEAN plus agreements would make the world's largest free-trading bloc. Trading among participating countries will have preferential tariff. Firms need to carefully check their benefits before exporting to ensure they are subject to the lowest possible trade barriers.

In addition, ASEAN is strategically located between two big economies China and India. ASEAN is the fastest growing region in the world with good fundamentals such as its long term investment is driven by a young population, it has growing middle class and its population is leading to urbanization.

The EU adopts a piecemeal approach to trading with ASEAN due to dramatic development gaps between countries as well as conflicting political agendas and an overall lack of cohesion. Cambodia has free access to EU under EU-GSP scheme already. Myanmar's transfer of power to an eclectic government in April 2011 was not recognized as free and fair by EU and EU has no plan to negotiate a free trade agreement with the country. EU is interested to have free trade agreement with Singapore, and Vietnam. Thailand's constitution makes any trade agreement a lengthy process. In addition, Thailand's political stability is also another hurdle to have trade agreement with EU.

Source: Cotroneo, C. (2010, May) Southeast Asia GLOBE, 39, 25-27

According to Dr. Surin Pitsuwan, former ASEAN secretary general, the number of middle class people in ASEAN has reached 200 million. This 200 million middle class people combined with the middle class in China, which has 400 million, and 200 million in India, East Asia will be the most attractive region for drawing foreign direct investment. Thus, firms in ASEAN need to prepare themselves for the influx of international investment by developing effective production process, giving more importance to social and environmental care which is increasingly stressed by investors worldwide. Practical insight 2.2 exhibits the benefits of ASEAN – China free trade agreement upon China's 12th Five-Year Plan.

ASEAN integration will encourage re-allocation of manufacturing industries. Thus, governments and enterprises

Practical Insight 2.2
Rising Chinese consumption will benefit ASEAN

China has started changing its growth model based on investment and export to high value manufacturing and demand. In January 2010, a free trade agreement between ASEAN and China took place. To date, about 90 percent of the products included in the agreement can be traded tariff-free. If China is going to increase domestic consumption, ASEAN will benefit.

China's 12th Five-Year Plan emphasizing on wage increase, spending less energy and focusing on manufacturing high value added products will shift production of cheap goods elsewhere and attract new technology. This will bring more investments from China into the least developed countries of ASEAN such as Cambodia, Laos and Myanmar. Similarly, focusing on high value added products will make China to seek new technologies, where Singapore is to play their strength. For example: Chinese textile giant Hodo Group plans to invest $320 million in Sihanoukbille Autonomous Port in Cambodia. Reallocating resources between China and Southeast Asia will make the products from the region more competitive.

The Chinese government has been making efforts to redistribute and balance the social income throughout China. The Chinese government policies have increasingly favored workers and their rights. In line with the government policy, Ministry of Human Resources and Social Security reported that a total of 30 provinces, regions and municipalities have raised their local minimum wages in 2010 with an average growth rate of 22.8 percent. This follows calls for higher pay at some foreign factories such as Foxconn and Honda in southern China. There are two options for foreign investors in China, whether to relocate their firms to lower labor cost regions in China or look for other low cost countries such as Vietnam, Indonesia. According to a report released by Aon Hewitt, a global human capital consulting company, there is a growing number of companies moving to China's western or central areas because of rapidly rising labor costs elsewhere. The Chinese new economic growth model; growth from within, plus 1.34 billion populations will increase confidence for investors that China is to move its growth pattern towards domestic consumption. This presents a great opportunity for multinationals of value added goods to transform their focus to China.

Source: China Daily Asia Weekly February-March 2011

in member countries need strong coordination to increase ASEAN's competitiveness rather than compete with each other. For example, rice export, under AEC, Thailand will lose competitiveness and market share within the region to Vietnam which can offer more attractive prices for white rice than Thailand. As a result, instead of competing, Thailand is to focus on high quality rice (Pratruangkrai, 2011). As part of the vision of the Malaysian government to become a developed nation by 2010, the government has announced a New Economic Model whereby the country will rely less on export growth but will instead focus on the service sector. (Pratruangkrai, 2010).

In addition, there are also some government trade policies which favor trade among nations. For example, the **Generalized System of Preferences (GSP)** scheme provided by developed countries to developing countries. The European Union, United States and other industrial countries initiated the GSP in the 1970s. There are currently 13 national GSP schemes notified to the United Nation Conference on Trade and Development (UNCTAD) secretariat. The following countries grant GSP preferences: Australia, Belarus, Bulgaria, Canada, Estonia, the European Union, Japan, New Zealand, Norway, the Russian Federation, Switzerland, Turkey and the United States of America (UNCTAD). GSP provides preferential tariff treatment (reduction or zero rated import duties over the Most Favored Nation Rates) on certain products originating in designated developing countries. This program is to increase export earnings and promote industrialization and economic growth in developing countries by providing market access of their products to developed countries.

Rules of origin are essential components of all GSP schemes. To qualify for the program, products exported from a GSP preference-receiving country need to fulfill the rules of origin of the respective preference-giving countries. All ASEAN countries except Singapore are beneficiary countries under many GSP schemes.

The following table 2.1 summarizes the coverage of GSP scheme for ASEAN countries. Traders need to find out more about the accessibility of their products to the particular country market they intend to export.

Thailand faces the possibility of graduating from the GSP program in 2015, whereby all tariff privileges would be revoked. This will make Thai products loose competitiveness in EU markets. Thus Thai government is trying to negotiate FTA with the EU. FTA with EU would establish a permanent GSP and would increase Thailand's competitiveness.

Trade Restrictions

Trade restrictions are generally classified as tariff restriction and non-tariff restrictions. Countries impose taxes on traded goods called **tariff restriction**. Taxes are imposed either as Ad Valorem[6] or Specific [7] or Compound[8].

Apart from taxes, other barriers which restrict trade are called **non-tariff trade barriers**. Non-tariff barriers can be further divided into: quantitative non-tariff trade barriers (quota) and non-quantitative non-tariff trade barriers. Non-Quantitative non-tariff trade barriers include the followings;

- Customs classification and valuation: can be very discriminatory since different rates are used for different categories.

- Antidumping duty[9]: is an additional tax imposed on imported products to counteract for the dumping[10] effect.

- Minimum import price limits

---

[6] Tariff in terms of a percentage of value of the imported commodities.
[7] Tariff in terms of a certain amount of tax imposed on each unit of export/import.
[8] Tariff rate which incorporates both ad valorem and specific.
[9] To be eligible for antidumping duties, one must prove dumping and domestic injury.
[10] Dumping means selling the goods in the foreign countries with lower than home market price.

Table: 2.1 Coverage of GSP scheme for ASEAN countries

Preference giving countries	Beneficiaries				
	Brunei	Cambodia	Indonesia	Laos	Malaysia
Australia		X		X	
Belarus	X	X	X	X	X
Canada	X	X	X	X	X
EU	X	X	X	X	X
Japan		X	X	X	X
New Zealand		X	X	X	X
Norway	X		X	X	X
Russian Federation	X	X	X	X	X
Switzerland		X	X	X	X
Turkey	X	X	X	X	X
US		X	X		

Table: 2.1 Coverage of GSP scheme for ASEAN countries (continued)

Preference giving countries	Beneficiaries			
	Myanmar	Philippine	Thailand	Vietnam
Australia				X
Belarus	X	X	X	X
Canada		X	X	X
EU	X	X	X	X
Japan	X	X		X
New Zealand	X	X		X
Norway		X	X	
Russian Federation	X	X	X	X
Switzerland	X	X		X
Turkey		X	X	X
US		X		X

Source: Author adopted from UNCTAD: Generalized System of Preferences, List of Beneficiaries 2009

- Countervailing duty: is an additional tax imposed on imported products to compensate for the subsidy[11] effect.
- Procurement policy: is forcing the exporter by the government to use the local materials or products up to certain percentage required by the government.
- Import licensing procedures
- Pre-shipment inspection
- Trade and labor standards
- Documentation requirements
- Trade related environmental measures
- Proportion restrictions of foreign to domestic goods (local content requirements)
- Etc.

The most recent non-tariff barrier is the carbon footprint of a product or service which is becoming an increasingly important issue for exporters and importers. Carbon footprint label indicates the total amount of Green House Gas (GHGs) emitted throughout the product's lifecycle. Carbon labeling

has become the requirement for exports to the EU countries. For example, from 2011 onwards, all products imported to France will be labeled with carbon footprint information. All airlines operating in the EU countries will need to limit and control their GHGs emission (The Nation, 2010a). The Excise Department of Thailand will also propose the government to impose a carbon tax on the retail price of diesel. The department also expects to collect a pollution tax on items such as air conditioners, batteries, pesticides, packaging, car tyres and lubricants, as well as on manufacturing plants (Chaitrong, 2011).   Practical insight 2.3,   2.4. 2.5 and 2.6 exhibit non-tariff barriers on trade.

---

[11] Import subsidy: domestic producers get help (subsidy) and can beat the foreign exporters. Export subsidy: the exporters get help (subsidy) and can compete successfully in the world market.

Utmost important document in international trade is the sales contract. Under most legal systems, international contract of sales comes into existence when a sufficiently precise offer by one party is accepted unconditionally by the other party. A sufficiently precise offer generally includes:
- A clear description of goods
- Price and payment terms
- Delivery terms, incoterms, including packing, invoicing, transportation and insurance instructions.

In the domestic trade, it is obvious that the rules governing the contract are those contained in the national law. As far as international trade is concerned, international sales contract or so called cross border sales contract, is governed by either the national law or an international treaty, the Vienna Convention on the International Sales of Goods (CISG).

Host government FDI related promotions are also another important factor to consider especially for export-manufacturers. The government promotions are discussed in the following chapter in detail.

Economic Environment

Economic attributes such as market size and market attractiveness, market growth, total population and location of population, income and wealth of people and gross domestic product (GDP) trend, level of inflation, level of employment, changing cost of production such as input- costs (wages and availability of cheap natural resources), labor productivity, interest rates and the like also influence the strategy formation of the firm. Firms also encounter different nature of competition depending on different economic settings such as whether they are operating under command economy, mixed economy or market economy.

Some other economic variables such as foreign exchange rate, foreign exchange volatility and convertibility also affect the trading businesses. For example, in the past, exporters have been very comfortable using the US dollar as their trade currency as it was perceived as stable and strong. Exporters prefer to receive their sales proceeds in the currency which is appreciating or at least stable. The US dollar has been depreciating against many of the world currencies since the past few years. If this depreciation of the US dollar is likely to be persistent, exporters who have been receiving less and less from their US dollar export proceeds are likely to use some other currencies like Yuan (if exporting to China) as their trade currency. Thus other factors that exporters need to consider are the choice of the appropriate currency of trading, and decision to hedge the trading currency and transferability of such currency as well.

Socio-Cultural Environment

Understanding the socio-cultural environment of the trading countries is also advantageous to the firm. Geographic distance, cultural distance such as social structure, language, education, religion, aesthetics, values, attitudes, manners, customs, physical and material environments make up the socio- cultural environment of the country. They affect the people's work ethic and desire for material possession. Thus for multinational managers, there is a need to develop cross-cultural literacy. High cross-cultural literacy could imply a firm's better understanding of its customers, is a very key to success. Thus cross-cultural literacy is critical to the success of international businesses. Practical insight 2.7 exhibits the importance of social and cultural factors in international business. Companies that are ill informed about the practices of other culture are unlikely to succeed in that culture.

Technology and Infrastructural Environment

Technology is vital for competitive advantage, and is also a major driver of globalization. One should consider the following factors in order to access the technological and infrastructural environment of a country:

Research and Development (R&D) Structure i.e. government spending, industry spending on R&D, level of technological development and related educational level, basic infrastructures such as transportation, communication, electricity and power supply, etc. Practical insight 2.8 presents the need of infrastructure development in the age of e-commerce.

Due to the differences in international market environments particularly in infrastructural environment, some products need product modification which properly meets market preferences. For example, Toshiba launched the power TV series- Power Saver, Power Charger, Power Booster- which are developed for the mass market in ASEAN where many areas in ASEAN have unstable power and signals (Ongdee, 2010).

Practical Insight 2.8
Waiting for the postman: Logistic industry hasn't caught up with fast development of e-commerce

China's logistic industry hasn't caught up with fast development of e-commerce. There is a big increase in online shipping orders in China. The country's largest online shopping site by volume has posted apologetic announcements to customers for the delay in deliveries. There are many privately owned express delivery companies in China and most of them are small and find it hard to increase the number of delivery employees and improve quality of staff. It may take three to five years for the industry to solve the problem. In addition, the recent shortage of diesel oil, which restricts the delivery vehicles' capacity and bad weather condition in North China compounded the delivery problem.

Source: China Daily Asia Weekly December 2010

Nowadays demographics have been changing, with the ageing group becoming bigger than ever in developed countries, creating more demand on healthy products. The drastically changing nature with more and more disasters make people more concerned about the environmental issues, thus creating more demand on green products. Digital material has also revolutionized the media resulting in fast information delivery and real time updates of events. Along with the revolution of the digital industry, E-commerce has been revolutionized. Consequently, multinational managers need to be aware of the changes in business environments.

Industry and Competitor Analysis

Industry analysis is a market strategy tool used by business firms to determine competitive intensity and attractiveness of market. Management needs to carefully analyze several aspects of the industry to determine the potentiality of the market. Analyzing the industry's economic factors, supply and demand, competitors, future market conditions and industry regulatory environment will help management decide whether to enter an industry. Economic factors of industry analysis include raw materials, expected profit margins and the interference of substitute goods. A supply and demand analysis helps management understand about the bargaining power of the consumers. The number of competitors is an important factor for a proper industry analysis. Management needs to know the existing and prospective local and global major competitors in the target market. The Porter five force analyses is one way to analyze the industry.

After thoroughly accessing PEST and industry analyses, firms can come up with existing opportunities and threats in that country. Thus firms can properly set the strategies to exploit the opportunities and overcome the threats. The following Table 2.2 (Threats, Opportunities, Weaknesses, Strengths (TOWS) matrix guides the firms to think about the strategy of the whole organization. By matching Strengths and Opportunities (SO) and Strengths and Threats (ST) the firm will come up with the strategies to use strengths to capitalize on the opportunities and minimize the threats. By matching Weaknesses and Opportunities (WO), the firm will also come up with the strategy to overcome the weaknesses by using opportunities and by matching Weaknesses and Threats (WT) the firm can minimize weaknesses and avoid threats.

Table 2.2 TOWS Matrix

	Opportunities (O)	Threats (T)
Strengths (S)	SO Strategies that use strengths to maximize opportunities.	ST Strategies that use strengths to minimize threats.
Weaknesses (W)	WO Strategies that minimize weaknesses by taking advantage of opportunities.	WT Strategies that minimize weaknesses and avoid threats.

Source: Author

Many firms are eager to tap the potentially profitable opportunities in the so-called emerging markets such as Brazil, Russia, India, China (BRIC) and countries in ASEAN. In April 2011, South Africa joined the club of the world's emerging economic giant BRIC. Now the club is called BRICS[12]. BRICS countries have the total population of nearly 3 billion from different continents (Richburg, 2011). However, caution should be taken in some countries where huge market potentials exist with poor infrastructure and lack of intellectual property rights protection.

Whether firms plan to handle international operations by themselves or collaborate with other firms, entering the global market needs formulation of strategies. In addition to the objectives and policies, and the firms' core competencies and external environments, proper formulation of strategies is critical. Many firms engage in international transactions by accident, not by proper design and plan. Such firms encounter a number of unforeseen problems due to

---

[12] BRICS aims at contributing significantly to the development of humanity and establishing a more equitable and fair world. In one of the first concrete steps, the five leaders agreed to have their development banks provide credit to one another, denominated in their local currencies and not, as is typical, in U.S. dollars(Richburg, 2011)

insufficient preparation and information. Efficient development of strategies can help managers avoid certain costly mistakes. Exporters can benefit from proper export strategies such as product pricing (taking into consideration transportation costs, export/import duties, insurance costs, banking costs, domestic price factors, etc), payment methods, export financing and so on. Importers can also develop proper sourcing strategy; seek for preferential duty treatment under the country of origin, duty refunds through drawbacks provisions, duty exemptions through bounded warehouse or free zones provisions, etc.

In sum, prior to entering the foreign markets, the basic fit between the product and the consumer preference is needed to be reviewed. A firm's internal analysis reveals the strengths and weaknesses of the firm and the market external analysis reflects opportunities and threats that exist in the target market. In addition, proper international business research (Strengths, Weaknesses, Opportunities, Threats (SWOT) analysis) together with development of good business strategies based on SWOT will make a firm successful. Practical insight 2.9 illustrates the SWOT analysis of organic vegetable export.

Practical Insight 2.9
Sample SWOT analysis of Organic Vegetable Export

Strengths: A firm's strengths are its resources and capabilities that can be used as a basis for developing a competitive advantage. For example, patents and strong brand name of the company, uniqueness of the product, the firm's bargaining power, product varieties, the firm's experience in the industry, international business experience, possession of health, food safety, photo-sanitary, Good Agriculture Practice (GAP), Good Manufacturing Practice (GMP), organic certificates and the like, company and product reputation, economy of scale and scope in growing, packing and distribution, good coordination among the firm's supply chain activities, relationship with the growers, cost advantages from proprietary R & D and know-how, resources and market and distribution networks.

Weaknesses: The absence of certain strengths may be viewed as a weakness. The nature of the product can be a weakness if there is long geographical distance between countries.

Opportunities: The external environmental analysis reveals certain new opportunities for profit and growth. For example, unfulfilled customer needs, loosening of regulations and removal of international trade barriers, support from government, a less competitive industry, market size and growth potential, favorable target consumers' life style, health consciousness of target consumers, favorable logistics and well developed infrastructure in both home and host country and price elasticity in the target market,

Threats: The absence of certain opportunities may be viewed as threats. Labeling regulations, a lot of non-tariff barriers such as requirement of certificates and documents, license requirements, foreign exchange fluctuations, unclear policies, rules and regulations, red tapes and corruptions are some of the examples.

Source: Author

References

- Agence France-Press. (2010, 21.7.2010). Google 'agrees' to respect China laws. *The Nation*.
- Chaitrong, W. (2011). Excise chief to propose carbon tax. *The Nation*.
- Demirbag, M., Ekrem Tatoglu, Keith W. Glaister. (2010). Institutional and transaction cost determinants of Turkish MNEs' location choice. *International Marketing Review, 27*(3), 272-294.
- Koch, A. J. (2001). Selecting overseas markets and entry modes: Two decision processes or one? *Marketing Intellignace & Planning, 19*(1), 65-75.
- Kumar, A. S., Erich A. Joachimsthaler. (1994). An interactive multicriteria approach to identifying potential foreign markets. *Journal of International Marketing, 2*(1), 29-52.
- Ongdee, S. (2010, 30.11.2010). Toshiba announces TV strategy for ASEAN. *The Nation*.
- Phatak, A. V., Rabi S. Bhagat, Roger J. Kashlak. (2009). *International management: Managing in a diverse and dynamic global environment* (second international ed.): McGraw Hill.
- Pratruangkrai, P. (2010). Malaysia to hike ASEAN investments: KL seeks developed-nation status by 2020. *The Nation*.
- Pratruangkrai, P. (2011). Rice Traders, Academics Agree on Need for Change. *The Nation*.
- Richburg, K. B. (2011). China, other developing BRICS nations seek change in global economic order. *The Washington Post*. Retrieved from http://www. washingtonpost.com/world/china-other-developing-brics-nations-seek-change-in-global-economic-order/2011/04/14/AFarMgdD_print.html

- Sakarya, S., Molly Eckman, Karen H. Hyllegard. (2007). Market selection for international expansion: Assessing opportunities in emerging markets. *International Marketing Review, 24(2)*, 208-238.
- Saquandeekul, S. (2010). Asean Strategic Plan of Action. Unpublished Seminor. Department of Trade Negotiation,Ministry of Commerce, Thailand.
- The Asean Secretariat. (2008). *Asean Economic Community Blueprint.*
- The Nation. (2010a). Carbon labeling: A barrier to Thai exporters? *The Nation Midyear Econmic Report, 27.*
- UNCTAD. About GSP. Retrieved from http://www.unctad.org/Templates/Page.aspintItemID =2309&lang=1
- Wood, V. R., Kim R. Robertson. (2000). Evaluating international markets: The importance of informaion by industry, by country of destination, and by type of export transaction. *International Marketing Review, 17(1)*, 34-55.

3   Export Import Promotion and Privileges

In order to achieve the economic goal of many countries, their governments offer different packages of trade promotions and privileges. In the early development stage of the county, development comes through substituting imported goods by local produced goods. Later export promotion is seen as complementary development strategy to import substitution. In the globalized world, many countries use export promotion rather than import substitution. Many countries promote export as it is the one of the sources of income for the country. Only a few counties such as Japan promote import as the country wants to weaken the currency.

In this chapter export promotions and privileges provided by the Kingdom of Thailand are discussed in detail. In addition, some of the promotional packages provided by less-developed countries in ASEAN such as the Lao People's Democratic Republic, the Kingdom of Cambodia, the Republic of the Union of Myanmar are presented. On contrary, export promotion offered by developed ASEAN County: the Republic of Singapore is also presented.

Export-Import Promotion in Thailand

There are three government bodies that offer promotion packages in Thailand, namely, Fiscal Policy Office and Customs Department, Industrial Estate Authority of Thailand (IEAT) and Thailand Board of Investment (BOI). Among various measures of the Thai government promotions, tax privileges are most extensively used to decrease cost of production and enhance competitive advantages for exporters.

The important measures implemented so far by Fiscal Policy Office and Custom Department are:

- Tax and Duty Compensation
- Duty Drawback or Refund under Section 19 bis of Customs Law;
- Duty Relief for goods placed under the Customs Bonded Warehouse scheme;
- Duty Exemption for goods taken into the Free Zones established by Customs;
- Gold Card Scheme; and
- Licensed Customs Broker.

The above measures provides the manufacturer exporter and trading agents of exporting goods with tax and duty refund, duty withholding, duty exemption incentives depending upon the type of promotion packages.

Depending on the types of promotion packages, there are certain formalities and deadlines the applicants need to meet to be able to enjoy the relief. For instance, in order to get the duty drawback or tax refund, the applicant must inform the custom department with the letter of intent for duty drawback before importation. To be eligible for the tax refund, imported products must have undergone production, mixing, assembling or packing then re-exported to a foreign port within one year from the date of importation. For detailed information, visit www.customs.go.th.

The main differences between duty drawback and bonded warehouse package are that in the duty drawback, the applicant pay the import tax on the imported goods and upon re-exportation, tax refund is requested. Since import tax is paid for imported goods, goods can be brought to anywhere for further processing. In the bonded warehouse, no import tax is required to pay on imported goods. Bounded warehouse allows importers to store the goods before re-exporting. For that reason, further processing should be done in the bonded area. Goods can be re-exported in the same nature or in the nature of processed goods. When the imported goods are taken for the domestic consumption from the bonded warehouse, import tax will be levied.

In addition to the tax refund and tax exemption, free zone package offers additional benefits, such as providing more favorable tariff assessment method. The duty on product manufactured abroad and imported into Thailand is assessed on finished products rather than on its individual parts, materials or components. Thai Customs lists a few main benefits that account for most of the companies that use free zone schemes as follows;

Relief from Import and Internal Taxes/Duties
Relief from Export Duty on Re-Exports
Relief from Standard/Quality Control Requirements
Duty Exemption on Waste, Scrap, and Yield Loss
Eligible for Export Tax Refund/Exemption Schemes

The comparative table between Free Trade Zone (FTZ) and bonded warehouse of the United States are shown in Table 3.3.

Another promotion package is provided by The Industrial Estate Authority of Thailand (IEAT). IEAT was established in 1972 as a government agency under the Ministry of Industry, and is responsible for industrial development and pollution control of industrial operations by setting up "industrial estates".

The government emphasizes industrial estates as an effective tool to spur and guide national industrial development, as a means to preserve and protect the country's natural resources because industrial estates make the enforcement of environment regulations easier, and as strategic hubs of revenue and career skills in provincial areas.

Firms operating in industrial estates/zone may be granted certain investment incentives such as permission to own land in an industrial estate, and permission to bring in

Table 3.3 Comparison of FTZ and Bonded Warehouse (United States) (Nelson, 2000)

Function	Bonded warehouse	Zone
Custom Permissible cargo entry	A bonded warehouse is within U.S. customs territory; therefore customs entry must be filed to enter goods into the warehouse.	A zone is not considered within custom territory. Customs entry is, therefore, not required until merchandise is removed from a zone.
Custom entry regulations	Apply fully.	Applicable only to goods actually removed from zone for U.S. consumption.
Permissible cargo	Only foreign merchandise may be placed in a bonded warehouse.	All merchandise, whether domestic or foreign, may be placed in a zone.
Customs bond	Each entry must be covered by either a single-entry term bond or a general term bond.	No bond is required for merchandise in a zone.
Payment of duty	Duties are due prior to release from bonded warehouse.	Duties are due only upon entry into U.S. territory.
Manufacture of goods	Manufacturing is prohibited.	Manufacturing is permitted with the duty payable at the time the goods leave the zone for U.S. consumption. Duty is payable on either the imported components or the finished product, whichever carries a lower rate.

Appraisal and classification	Immediately	Tariff rate and value may be determined either at the time goods are admitted into a zone or when goods leave a zone, at the importer's discretion.
Storage period	Not to exceed 5 years	Unlimited
Operations on merchandize destined for domestic consumption	Only cleaning, repackaging, and sorting may take place and under customs supervision.	Zone operations include sorting, destroying, cleaning, grading, mixing with foreign or domestic goods label, assembling, manufacturing, exhibiting, selling, and repacking.

Source: Nelson C.A (2000), "Import Export: How to get started in international trade" P.206

foreign technicians and experts. Moreover, firms operating in the Export Processing Zone (EPZ) which is one type of industrial zone, may be granted exemption from import duty, value added tax and excise tax on machinery and construction materials for the factory, on raw materials used in production. EPZ also grants exemption or tax refund for any goods (which are still qualified for such schemes).

There are a couple of factors to consider if investors decide to locate their factories outside the industrial estates. They are:

❖ Foreign investors do not have the right to own land, unless the company is specifically a Board of Investment promoted company.

❖ Investors also increase the burdens they must bear, namely
  ❖ have to pay for land preparation, filling and leveling.
  ❖ have to pay to gain access to utilities.
  ❖ have to build and operate their own water and wastewater treatment plants.
  ❖ have to ensure that the infrastructure will be adequate (For example, an industrial estate provides a 20 meter wide access road suitable for truck traffic.)
  ❖ have to worry about red tape, uncooperative local authorities, and corruption and criminal elements.
  ❖ cannot take advantage of opportunities to pool resources and form associations with industrial colleagues

Thus industrial estates are beneficial for manufacture exporters. Investment zones have long been used to support government goals in decentralizing Thailand's industrial base. In line with the government policy of decentralization from the Bangkok Metropolitan Area, the Board of Investment (BOI) has announced new "Policies and Criteria for Investment Promotion" since April, 1993, creating three Investment Promotion Zones[13] throughout Thailand. One key investment incentive set up by BOI is tax and duty privileges for promoted projects. Advantages of an Investment Promotion Scheme are listed as follows:

▪ Relief from/Reduction of Import Taxes/Duties (the extent of relief and reduction depends on location of the zone)
▪ Relief from Corporate Income Tax

---

[13] Investment promotion zones are divided as follows:
  Zone 1: includes Bangkok, Samut Prakan, Samut Sakhon, Nakhon Pathom, Nonthaburi and Pathumthani (Bangkok and 5 Provinces)
  Zone 2: includes includes Ang Thong, Ayutthaya, Chachoengsao, Chon Buri, Kanchanaburi, Nakhon Nayok, Phuket, Ratchaburi, Rayong, Samut Songkhram, Saraburi, and Suphanburi (12 provinces)
  Zone 3: encompasses the remaining 58 provinces

- Deduction of Transportation, Electricity and Water Costs
- Deduction of Project's Infrastructure Installation

BOI has three different zones and privileges differ from zone to zone. Recently in 2013, in response to the changing global and regional economic situation, BOI is revising its investment promotion privileges and strategies. The new BOI strategy will aim to promote competitiveness in development and value creation in the industrial sector and to promote green industry to facilitate balanced and sustainable growth. Thus, new BOI investment promotion privileges will be granted based on the merit of the projects such as environmental protection standards, location of the factory in the industrial zone or estate, and research and development program. Under the new system, evaluation process will be based on clear performance on key performance indicators, outcome of the project and cost-effectiveness of the investment. The current system of privileges based on zoning will be abolished (The Nation 2013).

Export-Import Promotion in Cambodia

The followings are some schemes provided by the Customs Department of Cambodia in facilitating export and import.

Temporary Admission (General Department of Customs and Excise)

Certain goods can be temporarily imported to be re-exported and are exempt from import duties and taxes. The importers are required to inform the authorities that such goods will be re-exported within the specified period and provide a guarantee which is refunded after all the obligations under the pledge have been fulfilled.

Deferred Payment System for Customs Duty and other Taxes (General Depart of Customs and Excise)

There is a deferred payment system for customs duty and other taxes. A security deposit or guarantee is required to cover duties and taxes of (a) temporary imports for re-exportation (which is refunded upon re-export), (b) goods cleared at Dry Ports, (c) temporarily imported sensitive goods (prohibited/restricted, high-tariff, or smuggling-prone) of investment firms, or (d) goods in dispute (i.e. with claims of exemption). However, there is no drawback system. A bank deposit is the acceptable form of security.

Bonded Warehouse (General Department of Customs and Excise)

Currently there are four bonded warehouses in operation in Cambodia. They are Meng Sreang Inland Port, CWT Dry Port, So Nguon Dry Port and Golden Ocean Dry Port, located within Phnom Penh. These bonded warehouses are used for storing and examining imported goods before they are released from Customs.

Additional information can be obtained at www.customs.gov.kh

Export-Import Promotion in Laos

The followings are some schemes provided by the Laos Customs in facilitating export and import.

Duty Exemption (Laos Customs): *Transportation through Foreign Territory and Goods in Transit;* will be exempted from export duty, and from exit and entry restriction rules.

Warehouse System (Laos Customs)

Temporary Importation and Exportation (Laos Customs)

Free Trade Zones (Kish Trade Promotion Center): Laos has no free trade zones, but the Ministry of Commerce has indicated that they are willing to establish many free trade zones throughout the country. Plans are currently underway for a free trade zone in Savannakhet province in southeastern Laos bordering with Vietnam.

Additional information can be obtained at www.laoscustoms.loapdr.net

Export-Import Promotion in Myanmar

Myanmar changed its economic system from a centrally planned into a market oriented system in late 1988. Since then, a series of structural reforms have been introduced which are designed to open up and integrate the Myanmar economy with the world economy under the Union of Myanmar Foreign Investment Law (FIL). The followings are some of the incentives given to foreign investors by the Foreign Investment Law (Ministry of Agriculture and Irrigation):

- Exemption from income taxes for up to three years
- Accelerated depreciation of assets
- Income tax relief on reinvested profits
- A reduction of up to 50% on income taxes due on products exported from Myanmar
- Exemption from customs duty on machinery and other capital goods imported as part of the operations
- Government guarantees against nationalization
- Repatriation of profits and invested capitals
- Carry forward losses for up to three years
- Exemption from customs duty on raw materials imported for the first three years of operations

Myanmar's export policy is to export all exportable surplus and diversify foreign markets by using natural and human resources. Increasing and diversifying exports and improving the quality of products are among the main objectives of the export promotion policy.

The registered exporters / importers are allowed to enjoy 100 percent export retention money for the import of goods. There exists neither export quota nor ceiling for any exportable product or any individual or organization. Regarding the import policy, import is allowed against the export earnings with a view to promote export and to overcome the balance of trade deficit problems.

License should be applied for any export or import. The validity of export / import license / permit issued by the Directorate of Trade is three months from the date of issue, and it cannot be extended. Export license fee is not payable on export of any commodity including agricultural crops. All the imports are subject to pay the license fees, customs duty and commercial tax and profit tax. Starting from 11th August 2011, commercial tax has been reduced from 5% to 0% and profit tax remained at 2% (Mizzima News, 2011b).

However, a lot of modifications and rectifications of custom law and foreign investment law have been taken place since the country opened up recently by late 2011. One needs to update the latest amendments in these laws when one does business with Myanmar.

Special Economic Zones: The Special Economic Zone laws were published in the Union of Myanmar on January 27, 2011. The laws offer tax exemptions for different sectors (5 years for production, 8 years for high-tech, 2 years for agriculture, livestock breeding and forestry, and 1 year for banking). The investor who invests and operates business in the Special Economic Zone[14]

---

[14] Special Economic will be at Daewi port and the six FTZs will be **Thilawa port** in Yangon, **Mawlamyine** in Mon State, **Myawaddy** and **Hpa-an** in Kayin State, **Kyaukphyu** in Rakhine state and **Pyin Oo Lwin** in Mandalay region.

(a) may apply for income tax exemption on the proceeds of overseas sale for the first five years from the day of commencement of the production or service;

(b) may apply for fifty percent relief on the income tax rate stipulated under existing law for the second five years on the overseas sale proceeds; and

(c) for the third five years, if the profit obtained from export sale is re- invested, may apply for fifty percent relief on the income tax rate stipulated under existing law on such invested profit.

Additional   information   can   be   obtained   at www.myanmar.gov.mm

Export-Import Promotion in Singapore

The Singaporean government constantly reviews the schemes and licenses to meet the needs of the traders. The following are some of the current customs schemes and licenses.

- Customs Schemes and License (Singapore Customs)
  - Temporary Import Scheme (TIS)
  - Licensed Warehouse Scheme
  - Zero GST Warehouse Scheme
  - Excise Factory Scheme
  - Industrial Exemption Factory Scheme
  - Petroleum Licenses
  - Air Store bond Scheme
  - Duty Free Shop Scheme
  - Apex License
  - Major Exporter Scheme (MES)
  - Import GST Deferment Scheme (IGDS)
- Inter-Gateway Haulage (IGH) and Barge Scheme (IGB)

- Container Freight Warehouse Strategic Trade Scheme
- Cargo Agents Import Authorization (CAIA)
- Company Declaration Scheme
- Bonded Truck Scheme
- TradeNet
- Free Trade Zones (FTZs) (Enterprise One)

Additional information can be obtained at www.customs.gov.sg

Practical insight 3.1 presents the effect of FDI promotional packages on price of the goods.

Practical Insight 3.1
Why made –in-China goods cost more at home.

Chinese travelling abroad shop for products such as iPads, laptops and cameras. Paradoxically, most of these products are made in China. However, they cost more in China. For example: "16 gigabyte iPads, assembled in Shenzhen, Guangdong province. Their launch price was US$499 (3,326 yuan) each in the United States and HKS3,888 (3,336 yuan) in Hong Kong. But when they were launched on the mainland a year later, each cost 3,988 yuan, at least 650 yuan more than abroad." the author explained. Theoretically, goods made in China should be cheaper in China. Export rebates on Chinese products are the main reason why goods exported from China are cheaper abroad.

China has a comparative advantage in processing and assembling products. To promote economic growth and solve the unemployment problem, the Chinese government grants tax rebates on the products that are exported. A rebate of 17 percent in value added tax means, a product is at least 17 percent more expensive in the domestic market than abroad. Taxes (VAT, consumption tax, custom duty) are paid if products are sold for domestic consumption. So products sold in China are priced high. In addition, the cost of the products' distribution at different levels of the sales chain is very high in China as the country's sales network is not fully developed. Finally, all these make branded products made in China more expensive in China.

Given the intense competition in the global market, export rebates on Chinese products provide subsidies to the products so that they can sell competitively in the developed countries.

Source: Han Qu who is a professor of economics at the University of International Business and Economies, Beijin, China Daily Asia Weekly December 2011

References
- Enterprise One. Export / Import : Free Trade Zone. Retrieved April, 2011, from http://www.business.gov.sg/EN/BusinessTopic/Import Export/DepositingNStoringYourGoods/imp_ftz.htm
- General Depart of Customs and Excise. Deferred Payment System. Retrieved April, 2011, from http://www.customs.gov.kh/deferredpaymentsystem.html
- General Department of Customs and Excise. Bonded Warehouse. Retrieved April, 2011, from http://www.customs.gov.kh/boundedwarehouse.html
- General Department of Customs and Excise. Special Import Processing Scheme. Retrieved April, 2011, from http://www.customs.gov.kh/temporaryadmission.html
- Kish Trade Promotion Center. Free Trade Zone. Retrieved April, 2011, from http://www.kishtpc.com/Free-En/free_laos.htm
- Laos Customs. Laws and Regulations. Retrieved April, 2011, from http://laocustoms.laopdr.net/laws_and_regulations_part4.htm
- Ministry of Agriculture and Irrigation. Business opportunities in Myanmar agriculture Retrieved April 2011, from http://www.myanmar.gov.mm/ministry/agri/business.htm
- Mizzima News. (2011b). Export tax reduced by three percent. from http://www.mizzimaburmese.com/news/inside-burma/7878-2011-07-05-10-11-28.html
- Nelson, C. A. (2000). Import Export: How to get started in international trade.

- Singapore Customs. Customs Schemes & Licences. Retrieved April, 2011, from http://www.customs.gov.sg
- Thai Custom Department. Custom Incentive Scheme , Retrieved April, 2011, from www.customs.go.th

4 Customs Formalities for Export and Import

Custom formalities are tied to all aspects of import and export transactions. At the export or import custom check point, product classification and valuation are common before doing custom clearance. Since, customs duty is determined by the classification code, classification of goods is of great concern for traders. To classify goods means to assign them a classification code in accordance with the existing regulations. Most countries classify goods in accordance with the harmonized commodity description and coding system known as harmonized system.

Harmonisation of Tariff Nomenclature

The Harmonised System (HS) is a system which classifies and describes products based on various criteria (i.e. a nomenclature). The World Customs Organization (WCO) created the system in an attempt to harmonize the description of products across countries so as to facilitate international trade. It comprises about 15,000 commodity groups. The HS system came into effect in 1988. Later this adaptation was widely used in most of the world nations. Amendments were introduced in 1992, 1996, 2002 and 2007. The next set of amendments will enter into force in January 2012. The HS replaces several classifying and coding systems that make statistical comparisons nearly impossible since different countries use different languages, descriptions, and coding systems in identifying the same products in different countries (World Custom Organization).

More than 200 customs, countries and economies representing more than 98% of the world trade use the HS. It determines, identifies or impacts:
▪ duty rates

- origin (change in tariff classification criterion)
- general import/export prohibitions & quantitative restrictions
- regulatory and licensing requirements (e.g. China Compulsory Certification (CCC))
- Commodity Inspection (including fumigation)
- antidumping, countervailing & safeguard measures
- the process of imports and exports
- basis of customs risk management and valuation audit
- trade statistic
- a comprehensive collection of data on the flow of goods between countries

In the Harmonised System Convention, thousands of products are classified under 22 sections and 99 chapters as follows(Exim Guru, 2010; United States International Trade Comission, 2011):

- 01-05 Live Animals and Animal Products
- 06-14 Vegetable Products
- 15 Animal or Vegetable Fats and Oils
- 16-24 Foodstuffs
- 25-27 Mineral Products
- 28 38 Chemical and Allied Industries
- 39-40 Plastic / Rubbers
- 41-43 Raw Hides, Skins, Leather and Furs
- 44-46 Wood and Wood Products
- 47-49 Pulp of Wood or of Other Fibrous Cellulosic Material
- 50-63 Textiles
- 64-67 Footwear / Headgear
- 68-70 Stone, Plaster, Cement, Asbestos, Mica or Similar Materials; Ceramic Products; Glass

- 71 Natural or Cultured Pearls, Precious or Semi-Precious Stones, Metals
- 72-83 Metals
- 84-85 Machinery / electrical products
- 86-89 Transportation
- 90-92 Optical, Photographic, Cinematographic, measuring, checking, precision, medical or surgical instruments and apparatus, clocks and watches, musical instruments, parts and accessories thereof
- 93 Arms and Ammunition
- 94-96 Miscellaneous Manufactured Articles
- 97 Works of art, Collectors' Pieces and Antiques
- 98-99 Special Classification Provisions, Temporary Legislation/Modification

Codes in digits beyond the two-digit level would represent further refinements to the description of the product (termed "sub-headings"). The Harmonized System only provides the descriptions up to the HS 6-digit level. This is depicted in the following examples for the HS Chapter 85 (Foreign Trade):

HS Code 85   Electrical Machinery and Equipment

85.17   *Electrical apparatus for line telephony or line telegraphy*

85.17.10   Telephone sets

85.17.20   Teleprinters

85.17.30   Telephonic or Telegraphic Switching Apparatus

85.17.40   Other Apparatus, for Carrier-current Line Systems

85.17.81   Other Telephonic Apparatus

85.17.90   Parts of Electrical Apparatus for Line Telephony or Line Telegraphy

Individual countries may extend an HS number to eight or ten digits for customs purposes and export purposes. The

HS consists of around 1200 four-digit headings and 5000 six-digit subheadings (Yu, 2008). The harmonisation would contribute to the smooth flow of goods across borders. In fact, even in the absence of any tariff reductions, harmonisation in these areas can help facilitate or increase the flow of trade. The significant rise in international trade and a more diversified pattern of trade have increased the need to simplify and harmonise these cross-border measures, and to restore customs administration.

Harmonisation of Tariff Nomenclature in ASEAN

Given the importance of customs harmonisation for facilitating trade, the seventh AFTA Council held in Brunei Darussalam in 1995 decided to turn this non-binding Code of Conduct into an ASEAN Agreement on customs cooperation. The current customs tariff nomenclature of ASEAN countries is based on the WCO Harmonized System (HS) Convention. However, ASEAN is currently working out a system that would harmonize its nomenclature systems beyond the 6-digit level (6th to 10th digit level) and is called the ASEAN Harmonized Tariff Nomenclature (AHTN).

Pre Tariff Classification

Some governments' customs departments provide importers with the pre tariff classification service. This provides importers with the ability to identify the correct tariff code prior to actual importation. This ruling system eliminates risks associated with declaring an incorrect tariff code. Practical insight 4.1 presents pre-tariff classification procedure in Thailand.

Practical Insight 4.1
Pre-tariff classification

According to the Thai customs department's rules, practitioners can submit a request to the Tariff Classification Bureau for a customs tariff specialist to determine the most appropriate tariff code. This process is completed by filling in the form Gor Sor Gor 1. This form, together with the supporting documents, must be submitted at least one month before importation. Supporting documents must also be attached with the request form to provide sufficient information as required by the officer to make a determination of the tariff code. The exact list of documents varies according to the characteristics of each imported product and explanation note for each tariff code. Some examples include trade names, specific product characteristics, production formula, chemical composition, production process, packaging details, samples, photographs and catalogues.

If there is sufficient information for the import practitioner to justify an import tariff code by himself, he can submit the proposed tariff code or comment on the classification to the customs department. The department will respond to the import practitioner's request within 30 days. The justification is free of charge and has not yet been binding per se in practice since it will need an effective legal notification to endorse.

Once the tariff code is determined by the officer, the importer can declare the product under the correct tariff code by attaching the tariff ruling letter with other import documents. The letter remains valid for one year after it is issued. However, the ruling letter will be void if the information concerning the product submitted is either incorrect or incomplete. If the result of the pre-classification request is not satisfactory, a new request can be submitted within 30 days after the tariff ruling letter was issued.

Source: Sitthichai Promsuwon works in the customs and trade group of Deloitte Touche Tohmatsu Jaiyos, The Nation, March, 2009

Harmonisation of Customs Valuation Systems in ASEAN

Customs valuation systems represent the method for determining the value of imported goods by a receiving country and are used for customs duties assessment, licensing requirements, taxes and other charges levied on imports. ASEAN member countries were committed to implement the GATT Transactions Value (GTV) method as stipulated in the *Agreement on Implementation of Article VII of the General Agreement on Tariffs and Trade 1994*, by the year 2000. This system is intended to be fair, uniform and neutral, and conforms to commercial realities, and which outlaws the use of arbitrary or fictitious customs values. Thus, ASEAN member countries now use GTV as a system of valuation.

In the GTV, customs value is established by using the *transaction value* of the imported goods, i.e. the price actually paid or payable for the goods being valued as reflected in the seller's invoice or other documents against which payment is made. The transaction value can also be adjusted by the addition of other charges including commissions, packing costs, proceeds of resale accruing to the seller, inland freight charges (paid to the seller), royalties, and license fees.

Where the transaction value cannot be applied, the following methods are used in sequential order of application:
- Transaction Value of Identical Goods (i.e., the transaction value of identical goods sold for export to host country)
- Transaction Value of Similar Goods (i.e., the transaction value of similar goods sold for export to host country)
- Deductive Value (i.e., the sale price of the goods in host country adjusted for costs incurred after shipment)

- Computed Value (i.e., value based on cost of production, general expenses and profits in the country of origin relating to the imported goods)
- Fall Back Value: The value is determined by customs and based on flexible interpretation of all the previous methods. Nevertheless, under this method, no customs value shall be determined on the basis of:
  o price of similar goods produced in host country;
  o A system which accepts the higher of the two alternative values;
  o Price of the same goods on the domestic market of the country of exportation;
  o The cost of production other than the computed value;
  o Minimum customs values; and
  o Arbitrary or fictitious values.

Harmonisation of Customs Procedures

Customs procedures represent another important administrative aspect of international trade. Though there are variations in customs procedures around the world, the following is the typical customs import procedure.

The customs import clearance process normally consists of various distinct steps (World Bank) :

1. Cargo declaration by carrier to Customs
2. Temporary storage of arriving goods
3. Customs import goods declaration
   - Preparation and submission of the goods declaration by importer/broker
   - Validation and acceptance of the goods declaration
   - Automated risk management/channeling

- Checking the goods declaration and supporting documents
- Assessment of the goods declaration by specialized customs officer (optional)
4. Physical inspection of the goods (optional)
5. Collection of duties/taxes by Customs (optional, by commercial banks)
6. Release of the goods by Customs
7. Delivery of the goods to the importer
8. Post-clearance auditing of importer by Customs (optional)
9. Pre-shipment inspection regimes

Export Clearance Procedures includes
1. File an Export Declaration
2. Preparing Supporting Documents such as
   - Invoice
   - Packing List
   - Foreign Transaction Form (if applicable)
   - Export License (if applicable), and
   - Other relevant documents (if applicable)
3. Check the Declaration and Supporting Documents
4. Collect Export Duties and Taxes (if any)
5. Inspect and Release Cargo

There are some restrictions regarding exporting and importing of certain products. For example, arts materials, cultural property, hazardous materials, plants and plants products, some kind of drugs, animals and animal products, etc. For exporting and importing of some products, one might need a license or a permit.

Trade conducted under the CEPT Scheme is not only governed by the standard customs clearance procedures for all goods but is also burdened by the additional requirement of determining the origin of the product. Goods originating from ASEAN can only be eligible for concessions if at least 40% of the value of its content is from ASEAN and this is certified by the issuance of the CEPT Certificate of Origin (form D). There is, therefore, a need to simplify and harmonize customs procedures in ASEAN in order to facilitate trade in ASEAN. For example, goods flowing across borders in ASEAN are subjected to three sorts of procedures 1) the certification of origin (form D), 2) export procedures from the country of origin (Export Declaration form is needed) and 3) import procedures from the importing country (Import Declaration form is needed).

Since most of the elements in the customs forms are similar, the procedure can be simplified by merging these three forms into a common ASEAN CEPT Form and ASEAN has formulated such a form called Asean Trade in Goods Agreement (ATIGA) Form D. ASEAN is committed to ensuring that these procedures are simplified and harmonised to promote transparency, consistency, efficiency and simplicity in its customs administration. ASEAN is also currently formulating a mechanism which expedites the clearance of CEPT goods. Some ASEAN members use the Electronic Data Interchange (EDI) system such as TradeNet® System in Singapore, and e-customs in Brunei. Many ASEAN countries have implemented the single window system for the expeditious clearance and release of cargo by customs.

Regarding temporary imports and exports of goods, countries use the **ATA** (Admission Temporaire – Temporary Admission) **Carnet system** which simplifies temporary importation of goods, professional equipments, and commercial samples. By presenting an ATA Carnet to foreign customs, the products and equipments pass duty free and tax free into a carnet country for up to one year. At the end of the year all the items listed on the carnet must be returned to the temporary exporting country. Certain goods cannot be covered by Carnets, such as perishable or consumable items. Diagram 4.1 shows ATA Carnet custom form.

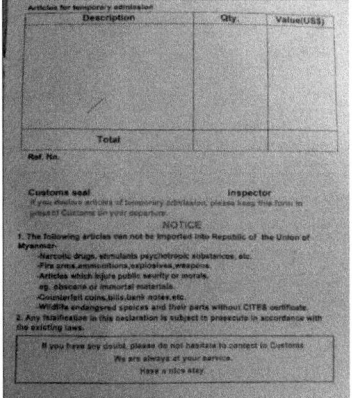

Diagram 4.1 ATA carnet custom form
Source: Author

The ATA Carnet may be used in the following countries:

Algeria	France	Lithuania	Singapore
Andorra	Germany	Luxembourg	Slovakia
Australia	Gibraltar	Macedonia	Slovenia
Austria	Greece	Malaysia	South Africa
Belarus	Hong Kong	Malta	Spain
Belgium	Hungary	Mauritius	Sri Lanka
Botswana	Iceland	Mongolia	Swaziland
Bulgaria	India	Morocco	Sweden
Canada	Ireland	Namibia	Switzerland
Chile	Iran	Netherlands	Taiwan
China	Israel	New Zealand	Thailand
Cote d'Ivoire	Italy	Norway	Tunisia
Croatia	Japan	Poland	Turkey
Cyprus	Korea	Portugal	UK
Czech Republic	Latvia	Romania	USA
Denmark	Lebanon	Russia	
Estonia	Lesotho	Senegal	
Finland	Liechtenstein	Serbia	

Tariff Structure in ASEAN Countries

Trading with many countries, traders need to understand the tariff structure of each country. Some country tariff structure is simple. For example, country such as Singapore imposes no import tariff but Goods and Services Tax (GST). Other country such as Thailand tariff structure is complicated. Import tariff structure in Thailand includes import tariff, excise tax and interior tax (for some products), value added tax, fees and charges. Understanding tariff structure of trading partner country will help traders' proper assessment of market.

Export Import Tariff

Depending on the trade agreement between country of origin and destination country, not all tradable goods are subject to tariff. Under the WTO agreements, countries cannot normally discriminate between their trading partners. Once one grants someone a special favor (such as a lower customs duty rate for one of their products), one has to do the same for all other WTO members. This principle is known as most-favored-nation (MFN) treatment. However some exceptions are allowed. For example, countries can set up a free trade agreement that applies only to goods traded within the group, discriminating against goods from outside. Thus imports from countries with which the host country has bilateral or multilateral agreements, preferential tariff rates are applied but countries with no bilateral trade agreement, MFN rates are applied. Visit the following website for the detailed MFN rates of 10 ASEAN countries; http://stat.wto.org/TariffProfile/WSDBTariffPFView.aspx?Language=E&Country=BN,KH,ID,LA,MY,MM,PH,SG,TH,VN.

The importers can choose to use the reduced import duty rate called **preferential rates** if they meet the conditions of certain privileges e.g. free trade agreement, GSP, BOI privilege, etc. Most tariff are with the Ad Valorem rates and some are with specific rates.

In addition to import tariff, some ASEAN countries impose value added tax (VAT) upon importation. Table 4.1(TMF Group) summarizes the VAT.

Table 4.1 VAT in ASEAN countries

Countries	VAT
Brunei	No VAT
Cambodia	10%
Indonesia	10%
Laos	10%
Malaysia	6% Service Tax
Myanmar	5%-30% Sales Tax
Philippines	12%
Singapore	7% GST
Thailand	7%
Vietnam	10%

Source: Author

Most ASEAN countries do not impose any export tariff; only certain goods are subject to export tariff and quota. The more detailed information regarding export import valuation, tariff, non-tariff information and export import procedure of respective countries are available at the following websites.

Brunei at   www.mofat.gov.bn
Cambodia at www.customs.gov.kh
Indonesia at www.beacukai.go.id
Laos at   www.laocustoms.laopdr.net
Malaysia at www.customs.gov.my
Myanmar at www.commerce.gov.mm
Philippines at www.customs.gov.ph
Singapore at www.customs.gov.sg
Thailand at www.customs.go.th
Vietnam at www.customs.gov.vn

Tariff Structure (Thailand)

There are three types of duties that any importer has to pay before the imported goods are released from the custody of Customs:

1. **Customs Import Duties**

   There are MFN duty rates or preferential duty rates for imported goods.

2. Excise Tax for Excise Department and Interior Tax

   An **excise tax** is set on selected number of goods (mainly luxury goods) including petroleum products, alcoholic products, cosmetics and cigarettes. Tax is based on an ad valorem or a specific rate whichever is higher. All goods subject to excise tax remain subject to VAT except tobacco and cards.

   Interior tax: called municipality tax is levied on products subject to excise duties at a rate of 10% of the excise tax.

3. **Value Added Tax (VAT)** for the Revenue Department

   General sales taxes or VAT is levied on most imported goods with exemptions only for published materials and books, unprocessed agricultural products, livestock, and agricultural inputs such as fertilizers and feed, and goods exempt from import duties under the Industrial Estate Authority of Thailand (IEAT) Act. In April 1999, the value added tax on goods and services was temporarily reduced from 10% to 7%.

In addition, other fees collected by the Customs Department include:

1. **Surcharges** under Investment Promotion Act; (not more than 50% of import prices)

2. **Fees** under customs laws such as attendance fees, overtime fees, customs seal fees, RTC strap fees, rent charge, etc.; and

3. **Fees** under other laws such as lighthouse fees under the Law of Navigation in Thai waters.

In Thailand, all imported products with value exceeding 1,000 Baht are subject to import duty and VAT at the time of importation except goods prescribed in the list of duty exemption of the Customs Act. Some of the imported products require an import license e.g. dangerous goods, food and health products, cosmetics, medical equipment, etc. Some other products are subject to non-tariff restrictions. The followings are some examples of non-tariff restrictions in Thailand.

- *Price control measures*: Antidumping duties
- *Technical Measure*:
    o Product characteristic requirements
    o Labeling requirements
    o Testing, inspection and quarantine requirements
- *Quality Control Measure*:
    o To protect human health: to import used motor vehicles, used six-wheeled buses (over 30 seats) and used imports of ceramic food containers coated with lead
    o To protect the environment: imports of plastic waste, parings, scraps, and used motor vehicles are subject to licensing requirements
- *Quotas*: 23 agricultural and agri-food products subject to tariff quotas.

- *Prohibitions*: To ensure national security: import prohibition applies to electrical or mechanically operated gaming machines in order to protect public morals
- *Temporary prohibition*: products from animal origin
- *License linked with local production*: Silk and Silk Yuan from China

Sample of Duty Assessment in Thailand (Thai Custom Department)

"*Company "A" imports goods into Thailand. The CIF value of the imported goods and applicable taxes and duties are as follows:*

- CIF value of imports   = 200 US$
- Import duty   = 60 %
- Surcharge/Special duty   = 10 US$
- Fee   = 50 US$
- Interior tax   = 10 %
- Excise tax   = 30 %
- VAT   = 7 %

How much should the total import duties and taxes be imposed on this import?

Calculation Method:

1. Import duty   =   (CIF value * rate of import duty) + surcharge
              =   (200 * 0.6) + 10 = 130

(*Note*: The amount 130 is to be used for calculation of excise tax and VAT.)

2.	Fee	=	50
3.	Excise tax	=	(CIF value + import duty + Fee) * {Rate of excise tax/1-(1.1 * Rate of excise tax)}
		=	(200+130+50) * {0.3/1-(1.1*0.3)} = 170
4.	Interior tax	=	Excise tax * Rate of interior tax
		=	170 * 0.1 = 17
	Base VAT	=	CIF value + Import duty + Fee + ExciseTax + Interior tax
		=	200 + 130 + 50 + 170 + 17 = 567
5.	VAT	=	Base VAT * Rate of VAT
		=	567 * 0,07 = 40

Practical insight 4.2, 4.3 and 4.4 exhibit customs rules on certain goods.

Practical Insight 4.2
PMTL welcomes latest ruling on cigarette case
The World Trade Organisation (WTO) delivered its final ruling on a tax dispute between Thailand and the Philippines that Thailand had violated the WTO rules "by subjecting imported cigarettes to VAT liability in excess of that applied to like domestic cigarettes". The Philippine government in 2008 petitioned the WTO that Thailand was conducting unfair customs practice by rejecting the import price declared by US-based Philip Morris for cigarettes it manufactured in the Philippines. Declared import price is used as a base for tax calculation, and Thai authorities suspected the company was declaring an artificially low price to avoid paying full taxes.
Source: *The Nation* June 19, 2011

Practical Insight 4.3
Government to set minimum prices for cigarettes
The Finance Ministry of Thailand approved the Excise Department's change in the tax calculation on cigarettes from factory prices to retail prices. The average taxes collected on imported cigarettes by the Customs and Excise Tax Department has lead to high retail prices.

Tax Types/ Rates	
VAT	7%
Excise Tax	79% of retail price
Excise Tax	376.19% of import price (CIF)
Local administrative tax	2.4%
Contribution to Thailand Health Organization	2% of stamp duty
Contribution to public television	1.5%
Import stamp duty on ASEAN goods	5%

Source: Finance Ministry

Source: The Nation March 15, March 18, 2011

Practical Insight 4.4: Duty Assessment in Thailand

Billing Details	
Entry No.: A022X560300106 Tariff:94052090	CUSTOM DUTY & IMPORT GOODS VAT 519.65
	DUTY HANDLING FEE (INFORMAL) 300.00
Value 56.00 USD 30.01 1,680.34	VAT 14.00
Frt. 132.60 THB 1.00 132.60	
Ins. 16.80 THB 1.00 16.80	
Duty 20.00 % 365.95	
Bur. 0.00 % 0.00	
Vat 7.00 % 153.70	
Total Duty 519.65	
Payment Terms	
Custom delivery unless	
stated otherwise in the invoice	
THIS IS A COMPUTER GENERATED INVOICE. NO SIGNATURE IS REQUIRED	Please Pay This Amount: THB 733.65

Source: Author

With regard to export from Thailand, all export products are exempt from export duty, except rawhide, wood and sawn wood. Occasionally, government put temporary restrictions on certain products in order to maintain country's political and economic stability. VAT for export is set at zero rate. Foreign trade transactions are subject to the provisions of exchange control laws and various licensing agreements too.

There are also many types of privileges provided by the customs department to the exporter in exporting products e.g. tax rebates, duty refunds for import materials and exports, manufacturing bonded warehouses, public bonded warehouses, etc as discussed in the previous chapter. In many countries, export shipments valued below a minimum requirement may not require a formal customs declaration. The exporter normally must sign an authorization paper (the power of attorney) allowing the customs broker or the forwarder to handle the customs declaration.

Tariff Structure (Brunei)

Brunei has the least number of taxes in the region. There is no personal income tax and there is no export, sale, payroll or manufacturing taxes. Based on the Income Tax Act 1949, only companies are subject to tax (Ministry of Foreign Affair and Trade Brunei Darussalam) .

Tariff Structure (Cambodia)

Import tax structure: Import duties are levied on any imported goods before releasing them from the custody of Customs except for goods receiving specific privileges that qualify according to the laws and regulations, whereby their duties are exempted. There are three types of duties and taxes that any importer has to pay before the imported goods are released from the custody of Customs:
- Customs Import Duties with an ad valorem rate
- Value Added Tax (VAT)
- Excise Tax for specific category of goods

Export Duty: There are four items of exported goods for which taxes have to be paid:
- Natural rubber
- Uncut (unprocessed) precious stones
- processed wood
- Fish and crustaceans, mollusks and other aquatic products

Tariff Structure (Indonesia)

Import tax structure: Duties and taxes which are applicable to imported goods in Indonesia consist of:
- Import duty
- Value added tax (VAT)
- Sales Tax on Luxurious Goods (STLG)
- Income Tax is 2.5% for a registered importer and 7.5% for an unregistered importer.

Export restriction: Indonesian customs classify products into products that are conditional of export regulations and of inspection, products not allowable for export and items allowable free for export. Details should be found at the Indonesia Customs Department website at www.beacukai.go.id.

Tariff Structure (Laos)

Import tax structure: All imported goods are subjected to customs duties and taxes. There are three types of duties that any importer has to pay before the goods are released:

- General imported goods: import duty + turnover tax[15]
- Luxury goods: import duty + excise tax + turnover tax
- Goods mentioned at No. 1 and 2 imported by persons shall pay the profit tax, in addition to turn over tax + excise tax.

Export duty: There are two types of Export duties that any exporter has to pay:

- Timber
- Unprocessed natural products
-

Tariff Structure (Malaysia)

Import tax structure: All goods dutiable on import are subject to customs duty in accordance with the Customs Duties Order of 1996. The types of duties are as follows:

- Import Duty
- Service Tax

Export Duty: Export duty is applicable to a particular type of goods.

---

[15] Turnover tax is similar to VAT or sales tax

Tariff Structure (Myanmar)

Import tax structure: With a few exceptions, all imported goods are liable to customs duties. Types of duties levy on imported goods in Myanmar are as follows:
- Import duties
- Commercial taxes[16]
- License fees

Export Duty: As for exports, tax is levied on export of a few commodities namely: rice and rice flour, rice bran, rice dust, oil cakes, pulses and cereals, bamboo and raw hides and skins. Exporters also have to pay 5% commercial tax and 2% profit tax from the export income (Mizzima News, 2011a, 2011b).

Export and Import are subject to the government license. Import shipment prior to the license date or arrival after the license has expired is not acceptable on arrival. Cargo may be fined or even confiscated (Masesk Line, 2011).

Tariff Structure (Philippines)

Import tax structure: All dutiable imports are levied on
- Import Duty
- Value Added Tax (VAT)
- Excise taxes are imposed on alcohol and tobacco products, petroleum and mineral products, automobiles and certain non-essential goods.

Export Restriction: The Philippines classifies export restriction into two categories; notable prohibited products and notable regulated products. Most export restrictions are set to help keep many of the Philippines natural resources

---

[16] Commercial tax is similar to VAT or sales tax

within the country and protect local businesses. Details should be found at the Philippines Customs Department website at www.customs.gov.ph.

Tariff Structure (Singapore)
Import tax structure:
- Import Duty: All dutiable goods imported into or manufactured in Singapore are subject to customs duty. There are four broad categories of dutiable goods in Singapore, namely intoxicating liquors, tobacco products, motor vehicles and petroleum products.
- Goods & Services Tax (GST)

Export restriction: There are very few controls on export from Singapore.

Tariff Structure (Vietnam)
Import tax structure: Types of duties and taxes payable on the importation and exportation of goods:
- Import duties
- Special Consumption Tax (SCT)
- Value Added Tax (VAT)
    - Goods that are subject to SCT are not subject to VAT.

Export restrictions: Permits and licenses are required for exports of a certain number of goods. Export duties are levied on many natural resources and commodities with a maximum rate of 45 percent. Some products are prohibited from exports such as antiques, logs and sawn timber, etc. Exports of rice and wood products (except for those exploited from natural forests) are no longer subject to government quantitative restrictions.

Nowadays with more and more trade liberalization, countries are reducing trade barriers. For example, Myanmar is in the process of economic reforms and government is ratifying the new laws including tariff and other taxes. Thus, one should visit respective country's custom website and study up to date tariff rates and tax structure.

References

- Exim Guru. (2010). Harmonized Code List, HS Classification Codes year 2007, 2006, 2005, 2004. Retrieved July 26, 2010, from **http://www.eximguru.com/hs-codes/default.aspx**
- Foreign Trade. Harmonized System Codes (HS Code). Retrieved April 2011, from **http://www.foreign-trade.com/reference/hscode.htm**
- General Department of Customs and Excise of Cambodia. Customs Tariff and Duty Rates. from **http://www.customs.gov.kh/#**
- Masesk Line. (2011). Export Service Restriction. from **http://www.maerskline.com/link/?page=lhp&path=/asia/myanmar/export/restrictions**
- Ministry of Foreign Affair and Trade Brunei Darussalam. Banking and Taxation. from **http://www.mofat.gov.bn/trade/invest/banking_and_taxation.htm**
- Mizzima News. (2011a). 2 percent left on export tax. *Mizzima News,* Retrieved from **http://mizzimaburmese.com/news/breakingnewsbrief/8147-2011-08-16-06-55-25.html**
- Mizzima News. (2011b). Export tax reduced by three percent. from **http://www.mizzimaburmese.com/news/insideburma/7878-2011-07-05-10-11-28.html**
- Thai Custom Department. Custom Valuation. Retrieved April 2011, from **http://www.customsclinic.org/index.php?option=com_content&view=article&id=147&Itemid=169&lang=en**

- United States International Trade Comission. (2011). By Chapter, Harmonized Tariff Schedule of the United States from **http://usitc.gov/tata/hts/bychapter/index.htm**
- World Custom Organization. Nomenclature. from **http://www.wcoomd.org/home_hsoverviewboxes_hshar monizedsystem.htm**
- Yu, D. (2008). The Harmonized System - Amendments and Their Impact on WTO Members' Schedules

5 INCOTERMS (INternational COmmercial TERMS)

Incoterms are the most commonly accepted terms of sales in international business. Incoterms define the mutual obligations of the seller and the buyer arising from the movement of goods under an international contract from the standpoint of risks, costs and documents. Incoterms are published and developed by the International Chamber of Commerce (ICC). Incoterms were first established in 1936. They are periodically updated with the latest version "Incoterms 2010". Incoterms 2010 is the eighth revision of Incoterms since their inception in 1936.

Purpose and Scope of Incoterms
- To define the importer's and exporter's costs, risks and obligations regarding delivery of the goods
- To provide universally accepted vocabulary
- To eliminate barriers caused by distance, language, and local business practices
- To eliminate uncertainties and different interpretations of trade terms on a world-wide scale
- To reduce risks of misunderstanding, disputes, and litigation
- To facilitate international commercial exchanges
- The transfer of property or titles of goods are not governed by Incoterms.
- Incoterms are not part of the contract of carriage (contract between shipper and the carrier).

INCOTERMS 2010 (Intenational Chamber of Commerce, 2010)
Incoterms 2010 principally cover;

- The transport cost that the seller will cover,
- The point at which the risk of loss will be transferred from seller to buyer,
- Who must handle customs formalities and pay duties and
- The responsibility for obtaining insurance coverage.

In any sales contract, it is important for the seller and buyer to agree on the terms of sales and know precisely what is included in the sales price. Exporters should choose the Incoterms that work best for their company. Traders should explicitly refer to three-letter trade terms (named place) followed by INCOTERMS 2010 when offering quotation or concluding the sales price on the commercial invoice such as FOB (Lamchabang) Incoterms 2010.

There are 11 Incoterms and they have been categorized under two categories.

Deliveries by any mode of transport (sea, road, air, rail) (These may all be used where there is no maritime transport at all.)

EXW: Ex works (….named place) Incoterms 2010

FCA: Free carrier (…..named place) Incoterms 2010

CPT: Carriage Paid to (…named place of destination) Incoterms 2010

CIP: Carriage and Insurance Paid to (….named place of destination) Incoterms 2010

DAP: Delivered At Place (….named place) Incoterms 2010

DAT: Delivered At Terminal (…named place of terminal) Incoterms 2010

DDP: Delivered Duty Paid (…named place of destination) Incoterms 2010

Deliveries by sea/inland waterway

FAS: Free Alongside Ship (.....named port of shipment) Incoterms 2010

FOB: Free on Board (.....named port of shipment) Incoterms 2010

CFR: Cost and Freight (....named port of destination) Incoterms 2010

CIF: Cost, Insurance and Freight (...named port of destination) Incoterms 2010

The following Table 5.1 and Figure 5.1 show Incoterms 2010 where risk and responsibility transfer.

Table 5.1 Chart of Responsibility

	Any Transport Mode		Ocean Transport Only			
Service	EXW	FCA	FAS	FOB	CFR	CIF
Packaging	S	S	S	S	S	S
Loading charges	B	S/B	S	S	S	S
Delivery to port	B	B	S	S	S	S
Export duty/taxes	B	S	S	S	S	S
Inspection of goods	B	S*	S	S	S	S
Origin terminal charges	B	B	S/B	S	S	S
Loading on carriage	B	B	B	S	S	S
Carriage charges	B	B	B	B	S	S
Insurance	B	B	B			S
Destination unloading charges	B	B	B	B	S/B	S/B
Delivery to destination	B	B	B	B	B	B
Import custom duty/taxes	B	B	B	B	B	B

Table 5.1 Chart of Responsibility (continued)

Service	Any Transport Mode				
	CPT	CIP	DAT	DAP	DDP
Packaging	S	S	S	S	S
Loading charges	S	S	S	S	S
Delivery to port	S	S	S	S	S
Export duty/taxes	S	S	S	S	S
Inspection of goods	S	S	S	S	S
Origin terminal charges	S	S	S	S	S
Loading on carriage	S	S	S	S	S
Carriage charges	S	S	S	S	S
Insurance		S			
Destination unloading charges	S	S	B	S**/B	S**/B
Delivery to destination	B	B	B	S	S
Import custom duty/taxes	B	B	B	B	S

S = seller, B = Buyer
S * if mandated by the government of the exporting country or else by buyer
S ** if unloading charges incur at the place of destination which are covered under the contract of carriage, the seller is not entitled to recover such costs from the buyer unless otherwise agreed between parties.
Source: Author

EXW: EX WORKS (.....named place) Incoterms 2010 (Intenational Chamber of Commerce, 2010)

- The seller must deliver the goods by placing them at the disposal of the buyer at the agreed point on the sales contract usually outside the seller's premises.
- Seller does not have to clear for export and load on any collecting vehicle.
- The buyer pays all transportation costs and also bears all risks for bringing the goods from the seller's premises to their final destination. This term requires that the buyer must be able to carry out export formalities in the country of export.

- Risks are transferred from the seller to the buyer, when the goods have been placed at the disposal of the buyer.

FCA: FREE CARRIER (.....named place) Incoterms 2010 (Intenational Chamber of Commerce, 2010)
- The seller delivers the goods into the custody of the first carrier nominated by the buyer at the named place, and this is where risk passes from seller to buyer. The seller has no obligation to the buyer to make a contract of carriage and contract of insurance.
- If delivery occurs at the seller's premises, the seller is responsible for loading on the means of transport provided by the buyer.
- If delivery occurs at any other place, the seller is not responsible for unloading from the seller's means of transport and loading on the means of transport provided by the buyer.
- FCA requires the seller to clear the goods for export, where applicable.
- Risks are transferred when the goods have been delivered to the first carrier.

CPT: CARRIAGE PAID TO (...named place of destination) Incoterms 2010 (Intenational Chamber of Commerce, 2010)
- The seller delivers the goods to the carrier or another person nominated by the seller at an agreed place.
- The seller pays the cost of carriage necessary to bring the goods to the named destination. The seller also pays the cost of loading the goods at the origin and any charges for unloading at the place of destination.
- The passing of risk from the seller occurs when the goods have been delivered into the custody of the first carrier. If

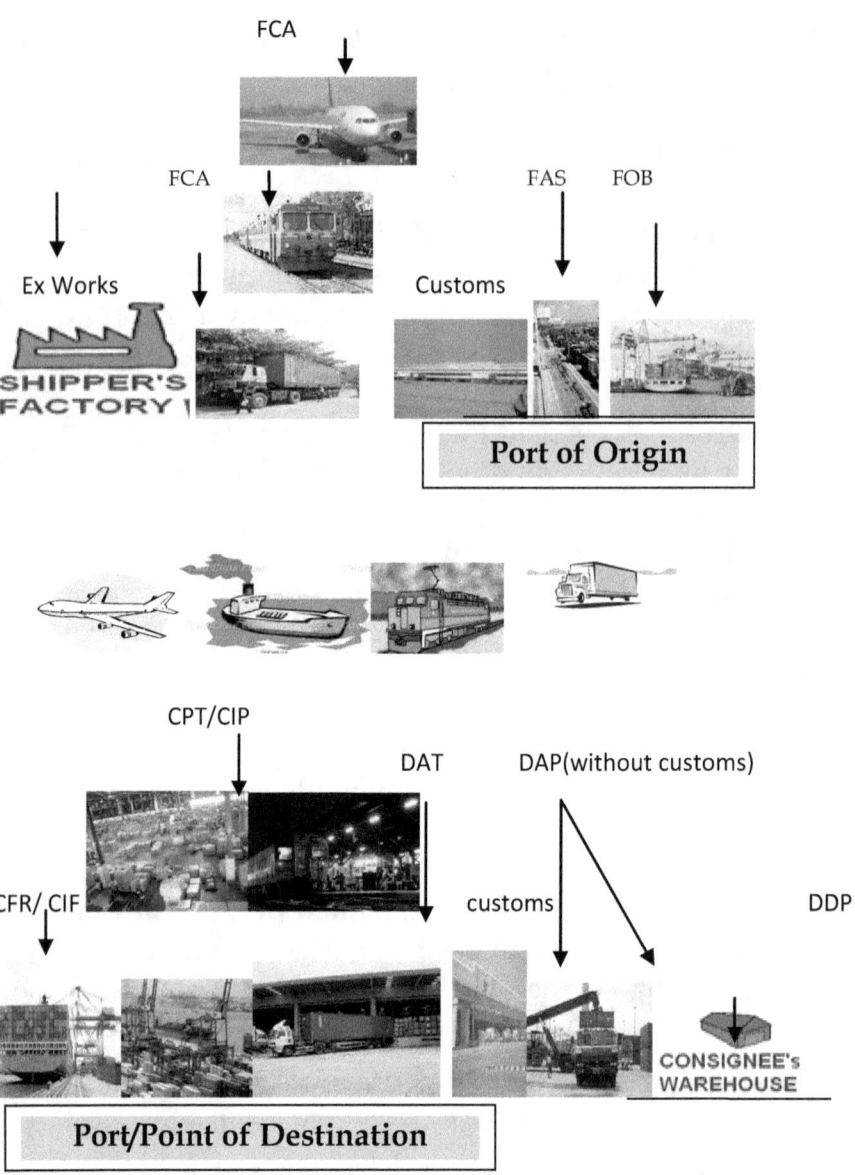

Figure 5.1 Incoterms 2010

Source: Author

subsequent carriers are used for the carriage to the agreed destination, the risk passes when the goods have been delivered to the first carrier.

- CPT requires the seller to clear the goods for export, where applicable and the buyer must pay all import duties, taxes and other charges of carrying out import customs formalities.

- Carrier means any person who, in a contract of carriage, undertakes to perform or to procure the performance of transport, by rail, road, air, sea, inland waterway or by a combination of such modes.

CIP: CARRIAGE AND INSURANCE PAID TO (...named place of destination) Incoterms 2010 (Intenational Chamber of Commerce, 2010)

- The seller delivers the goods to the carrier or another person nominated by the seller at an agreed place.

- The seller pays the cost of carriage necessary to bring the goods to the named destination. The seller also pays the cost of loading the goods at the origin and any charges for unloading at the place of destination.

- The seller also obtains contracts for insurance cover against the buyer's risk of loss of or damage to the goods during the carriage. The buyer should note that under the CIP term the seller is required to obtain insurance only on minimum cover.

- Should the buyer wish to have the protection of greater cover, he would either need to agree with the seller or to make his own extra insurance arrangements.

- The passing of risk from the seller occurs when the goods have been delivered into the custody of the first carrier.

- If subsequent carriers are used for the carriage to the agreed destination, the risk passes when the goods have been delivered to the first carrier.
- CIP requires the seller to clear the goods for export where applicable and the buyer must pay all import duties, taxes and other charges of carrying out import customs formalities.

DAT: DELIVERED AT TERMINAL (...named terminal) Incoterms 2010 (Intenational Chamber of Commerce, 2010)
- The seller delivers the goods at the disposal of the buyer at a named port or place of destination once unloaded from the arriving means of transport.
- Terminal includes quay, warehouse, container yard or road, rail or air terminal,
- Both parties should agree about the terminal and if possible a point within the terminal where the risk transfers from the seller to the buyer should be agreed.
- Thus the seller is responsible for the costs and risks of bringing the goods to the agreed point at the terminal unloaded.
- The seller is responsible for the export clearance procedures, however, the importer is responsible for import procedures and formalities including paying import duty if it is applicable.
- However, if the parties wish the seller to be responsible for all the cost and responsibilities from the terminal to another point, DAP or DDP term should be used.

DAP: DELIVERED AT PLACE (..... named place) Incoterms 2010 (Intenational Chamber of Commerce, 2010)

- It means that the seller delivers the goods at the disposal of the buyer on the arriving means of transport ready for unloading at the agreed place of destination.
- Both parties should agree as clearly as possible the point within the agreed place of destination as this is the point where the risk transfers from the seller to the buyer.
- Thus the seller is responsible for the costs and risks of bringing the goods to the agreed point.
- If the seller incurs unloading costs at the agreed place of destination, they are not entitled to recover by the buyer unless previously agreed or else unloading charges are paid by the buyer.
- The seller is responsible for the export clearance procedures, however, the importer is responsible for import procedures and formalities including paying import duty if it is applicable.
- However, if the parties wish the seller to be responsible for clearing the goods, applying the duties, etc.., DDP term should be used.

DDP: DELIVERED DUTY PAID (....named place of destination) Incoterms 2010 (Intenational Chamber of Commerce, 2010)

- The seller delivers the goods at the disposal of the buyer, clears for import, and is ready for unloading from any arriving means of transport at the named place of destination.
- The seller has to bear all the costs and risks involved in bringing the goods thereto including, where applicable, any duty (which term includes the responsibility for and

the risk of the carrying out of customs formalities and the payment of formalities, customs duties, taxes and other charges) for import in the country of destination.

- If the seller incurs unloading costs at the agreed place of destination, they are not entitled to recover by the buyer unless previously agreed or else unloading charges are paid by the buyer.
- The EXW term represents the minimum obligation for the seller; DDP represents the maximum obligation for the seller.
- DDP should not be used if the seller is unable directly or indirectly to obtain the import license.
- However, if the parties wish to exclude from the seller's obligations some of the costs payable upon import of the goods (such as value-added tax-VAT), this should be made clear by adding explicit wording to this effect in sale contract.

FAS: FREE ALONGSIDE SHIP (...named port of shipment) Incoterms 2010 (Intenational Chamber of Commerce, 2010)

- The seller delivers the goods alongside the vessel nominated by the buyer at the port of shipment. This means that the buyer has to bear all costs and risks of loss of or damage to the goods from that moment. The passing of risk occurs when the goods have been delivered to the quay at the port of shipment.
- The parties need to clearly specify the loading point at the named port of shipment as the cost and risk to that point are taken by the seller and the costs and associated handling charges may vary according to the practice of the port.

- Where the goods are in containers, it is typical for the seller to hand the goods over to the carrier at a terminal and not alongside the vessel. In such situations, the FAS rule would be inappropriate, and the FCA rule should be used.
- FAS requires the seller to clear the goods for export.
- This is a reversal from previous incoterms 1990 versions which required the buyer to arrange for export clearance.

FOB: FREE ON BOARD (...named port of shipment) Incoterms 2010 (Intenational Chamber of Commerce, 2010)
- The seller delivers the goods on board the vessel nominated by the buyer at the port of shipment. This means that the buyer has to bear all costs and risks of loss of or damage to the goods from that moment. The passing of risk occurs when the goods have been delivered on board the vessel.
- FOB may not be appropriate where goods are handed over to the carriers before they are on board the vessel, for example goods in containers which are typically delivered at the terminal. In such situations, the FCA rule should be used.
- The FOB term requires the seller to clear the goods for export.
- The buyer pays freight, insurance, unloading costs and transportation from the port of origin to the buyer's factory.

CFR: COST AND FREIGHT (...named port of destination) Incoterms 2010 (Intenational Chamber of Commerce, 2010)
- The seller delivers the goods on board the vessel at the port of shipment on the date or within the agreed period.

- The seller must obtain logistic service contract and pay the cost and freight necessary to bring the goods to the named port of destination. The risk of loss of or damage to the goods as well as any additional costs are transferred from the seller to the buyer once the goods are on board the vessel.
- Cost of loading the goods on board at the port of shipment and any charges for unloading at the agreed port of discharge are for the seller's account under the contract of carriage.
- Unloading charges such as lighterage and wharfage charges, unless they are in the seller's account under contract of carriage, are paid by the buyer.
- CFR term requires the seller to clear the goods for export. The seller is responsible for export customs formalities. The importer is responsible for import formalities and duties.

CIF: COST INSURANCE AND FREIGHT (....named port of destination) Incoterms 2010 (Intenational Chamber of Commerce, 2010)
- Risks and responsibilities of seller and buyer in CIF term are the same as those of CFR.
- However, in CIF the seller also has to procure marine insurance against the buyer's risk of loss of or damage to the goods during the carriage.
- Consequently, the seller obtain contract for insurance and pays the insurance premium.
- The buyer should note that under the CIF term the seller is required to obtain insurance only on minimum cover.

- Should the buyer wish to have the protection of greater cover, he would either need to agree with the seller or to make his own extra insurance arrangements.
- The CIF term requires the seller to clear the goods for export. The seller is responsible for export customs formalities. The importer is responsible for import formalities and duties.

Variants of Incoterms (Internatinal Chamber of Commerce, 2003)

In practice, it frequently happens that the parties seek further precision than the term could offer by adding words to an Incoterm called variants of Incoterms. When such words are added, it is necessary to clarify in the contract of sale whether the added obligations are only related to costs or both costs and risks.

The examples of variants of Incoterms are

FOB stowed and trimmed means the added obligation for the seller to perform stowage and/or trimming of the goods on board the ship.

EXW loaded means the added obligation for the seller to load the goods on the buyer's collecting vehicle.

EXW cleared means the seller clears at the customs.

CFR/CIF landed means the seller incurs cost of discharging.

Theory and Practice of Incoterms (Internatinal Chamber of Commerce, 2003)

There are differences theoretical Incoterms and actual practices regarding with incoterms. The seller should not be surprised with the difference between the theoretical Incoterms and daily practices. The followings are some of the examples.

In theory, under **FOB** contracts, the buyer should inform the seller of the name of the ship and its date of arrival at the port of loading. In practice, many buyers do not want to do so and the sellers must select a ship and load the goods on their behalf.

In the case in **CIF** shipments, marine risks are borne by the buyer and the buyer should be the one who claims the compensation from the insurance company in the event of loss and or damage. However, in practice, in many cases, it is the seller who makes the claim on behalf of the buyer.

If there are any disputes arising out of the differences, the seller should learn that they can be settled by the Rules of Arbitration of the International Chamber of Commerce.

Other Points to Remember

The importer will be wise to describe precisely the point of delivery as failure to do so will allow the exporter to exploit general terms. For example, "FOB Thailand" will ultimately allow the exporter to deliver at any ports in Thailand.

D terms allow for greater control of the quality of transport by the seller. In case of high-value manufactured goods, it may be very important for the seller to be in position o assure that the goods arrive in time and in good condition. Control of the entire transport chain is facilitated for the seller under D-terms. Moreover, in highly competitive markets, the buyers may insist on being quoted D-terms which facilitate the comparison of offers from different countries.

In general, cost of transportation decline according to the amount or the volume of transport service purchased. Thus, the total cost of transport between seller and buyer will in general be cheaper if it is arranged entirely by the seller or the buyer. This implies that using EX-work or D-terms will have comparatively more favorable transport cost.

An inexperienced exporter may want to use the Ex Works as it carries the least burden for the exporter. The most burdens to the exporter is the DDP term. Thus, it is not recommended for the companies that are new to export.

Custom clearance obligation not only includes the payment of duty and other charges but also the performance and payment of whatever administrative matters are connected with the passing of the goods through customs and the information to the authorities in this connection.

In choosing the appropriate Incoterms, many details such as tariff and non-tariff barriers and trade regulations, currency exchange, service providers' reputation are needed to be taken into consideration.

Incoterms and Liner Terms (Internatinal Chamber of Commerce, 2003)

Incoterms is a contract of sales made between shipper (exporter) and the consignee (importer). Liner term is specified in the contract of carriage. It is a contract between shipper and the carrier (shipping line). The ICC Commission on Marine Transport has undertaken a study to determine the feasibility of establishing standard liner terms (shipping terms). Though not yet formally established as standard liner terms, the following shipping terms are of international usage.

Gate Term: The term which imposes the least obligation on the contracting shipper: the shipper merely delivers the goods on a means of transport to the unloading point.

Warehouse Term: The contracting shipper delivers the goods in a warehouse in the port. At discharge, the carrier delivers the goods to the consignees in a warehouse in the port of destination.

Tackle Term: The contracting shipper delivers the goods to the carrier on the quay in the port of loading. In the port of discharge, the carrier delivers the goods to the consignee on the quay, unloaded from the vessel.

Under ship's tackle
- Loading – the shipper must bring the goods directly under the crane or platform which will hoist the goods on board.
- Unloading – the carrier will unstow the goods and place them on the ship's deck; all other operations including lowering the goods to the quay and sorting them, are for the shipper or consignee.

Under Ship quay
- Loading – the carrier's responsibility extends to loading goods brought anywhere within the area alongside the ship.
- Unloading – the carrier's responsibility includes lowering the goods to the quay, sorting the goods into different consignments, and in some cases, storage under cover or in shed.

Ship Term: The contracting shipper delivers the goods on board the vessel. At discharge, goods are delivered on board the vessel in the port of destination. On board is also called 'free in', 'free out' or 'free in and out'.
- Loading – free in – the carrier only makes the ship available. The shipper must hoist the goods on board and stow them in the ship's hold.
- Unloading – free out – the carrier only brings the ship alongside the quay; the shipper or consignee pay for having the goods unstowed and lowered to the quay.
- Free in and out – under this variation, the carrier will handle only the stowing and unstowing of the goods.

In many cases, private contractors called stevedores will take care of all cargo handling operations and will bill them, according to the particular shipment, to the carrier, the shipper or the consignee.

References
- Intenational Chamber of Commerce. (2010). *Incoterms 2010: ICC Rules for the Use of Domestic and International Trade Terms*: ICC Services.
- Internatinal Chamber of Commerce. (2003). *Guide to Export-Import Basics* (second ed.): ICC Publishing.

6 Export Import Documentation

Globalization and trade liberation agreements among countries reduce tariff barriers, on the other hand, concerns regarding global warming, human rights, health and safety issues have been paid more attention. Thus today trading atmosphere demands more certifications and documents by different departments such as food and drug administration, department of fisheries, forestry department. It is important that the trader is familiar with those certifications, documents and the languages used in export import documentation. The following terminologies are introduced for the readers.

In Contract of Sales
    Exporter – Seller
    Importer – Buyer
In Transport Documents
    Exporter – Shipper, consignor
    Importer – Receiver, Consignee
    Transport Service Provider – Customs Broker, Freight Forwarder, Carrier, Liner
In Bill of Exchange
    Exporter – Drawer
    Importer – Drawee
In Letter of Credit
    Exporter – Beneficiary
    Importer – Applicant
Banks involved are
    Importer's bank: Issuing bank
    Exporter's bank: Advising bank, and /or Confirming bank

Throughout the export import process, there are many sets of documents requested at different places. To know the proper documents flow throughout the export import process, it is needed to understand the export import procedure first. The following Figure 6.1 illustrates the typical export import procedures using letter of credit as a payment method.

1. Seller and buyer conclude a sales contract, with a certain method of payment usually by documentary Letter of Credit (L/C).
2. Buyer (applicant) applies L/C at his bank, usually in the buyer's country, in favor of the seller (beneficiary).
3. Buyer's bank (issuing bank) issues the L/C and requests another bank, usually a correspondent bank in the seller's country, to advice, and/or to confirm the credit.
4. Advising bank forwards letter of credit to the seller informing about the terms and conditions of credit.
5. If credit terms and conditions conforms the sales contract, the seller prepares goods and arranges for the delivery of goods to carrier. The seller receives bill of lading (B/L) from the carrier in exchange for the goods.
6. Seller prepares the documents requested in the letter of credit. Together with those documents and documents evidencing the shipment, B/L, the seller presents the draft (bill of exchange) to the paying, accepting or negotiating bank named in the credit (usually to the advising bank).
7. Bank, other than the issuing bank, sends the documents and draft to the issuing bank.
8. Bank examines the documents and draft whether they are in compliance with the L/C terms. If all the conditions are complied with the L/C, the seller's draft is honored which means the bank will pay, accept or negotiate.
9. Documents are released to the buyer by the issuing bank after payment from the buyer, or on other terms agreed between the bank and buyer.
10. Buyer surrenders the delivery order or bill of lading to the carrier (in case of ocean freight) in exchange for the goods.

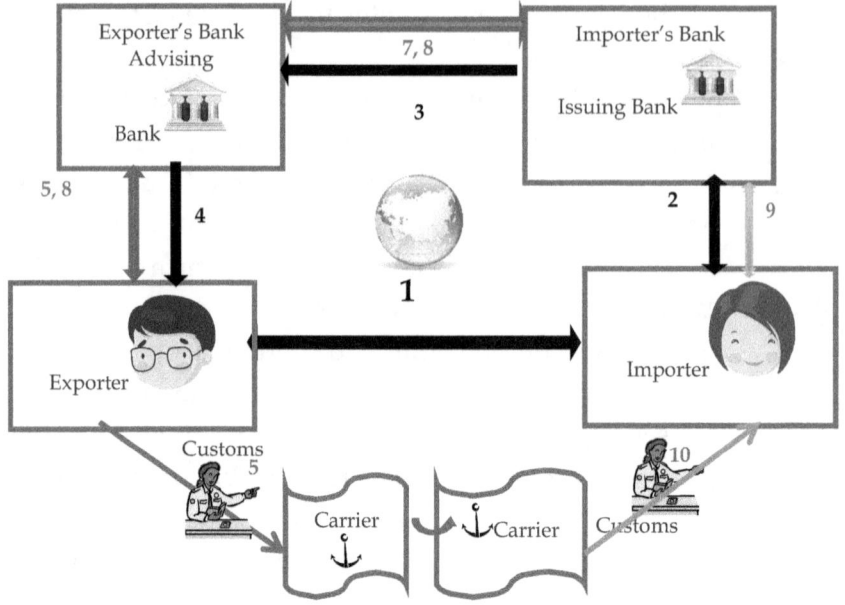

Figure 6.1 Typical Export Import Procedures
Source: Author

The followings are some of the important documents used in export import process.

Export Import Documentation

Pro forma Invoice or Sales Contract: is basically an advance copy of the commercial invoice. It specifies the product, price, quantity, delivery and the payment terms. The seller acknowledges the buyer's purchase order by issuing pro forma invoice. The pro forma invoice is often used by the importer for the import license permission purpose, L/C opening purpose and foreign exchange (import) allocation.

The use of the standard contract form is quite common in international trade. The ICC model contracts are currently available for international trade. The ICC model contracts respond to the need of international traders for a neutral, uniform framework for the contractual dealing. The application can be found at **http://www.iccwbo.org/policy/law/id272/index.html**. The sample of the ICC Model International Sale Contract can be seen in the appendix.

Traders should be aware of the danger of contracts based on a "handshake" or a "gentlemen's agreement". When dispute arises, reference to the contract is the first recourse of the parties. International contracts should provide clear and detailed stipulations regarding documentary obligations and traders should not sign contracts without reading them and understanding the stipulated terms and conditions in the contract. Moreover, traders should not let sales personnel sign purchase orders without management review as well.

Breach of a contract and the remedies: A contract may or will specify that a party which fails to comply with obligations, or is late in doing so, will provide certain remedies. Most legal systems make all of the following remedies available to some extent, depending on the circumstances of a particular case: money damages, termination and/or specific performance. Under most systems of the law, a party can be excused from a failure to perform a contract obligation that is caused by the totally unforeseeable events such as outbreak of war. In such cases, the importer may buy additional clauses in the insurance policy.

Late delivery of some products such as nonperishable products, is not a cause of concern, and the payment of a small percentage penalty by the exporter in such cases seems reasonable. However, with other products, late delivery is a serious breach, depriving the importer of the entire value of the product. In such cases, the importer will want to insist in the contract that time of delivery is "of essence". The importer may further wish to make the exporter liable for some sequential damages following late delivery.

The remedies for a breach of contract will vary according to the following:
- Terms of contract – the contract may itself specify particular remedies.
- Applicable law – national legal systems have different approaches to particular remedies. For example, civil law courts are more receptive to the application of specific performance remedy.
- The nature and gravity of the breach – remedies also depend on the characteristics of the breach. In general, most legal systems seek to avoid creating harsh remedies for minor breaches. The two concepts in this regard are:
  o Substantial performance – if the party (exporter) has performed the bulk of his obligations, but has failed to perform only to a small degree or unimportant matters, then the aggrieved party may only be allowed the remedy of a price reduction.
  o Fundamental breach – if the breach is substantial that deprives the aggrieved party of the intended benefit of the contract, the aggrieved party may be allowed to terminate the contract.

Commercial Invoice: is a record or evidence of transaction between the exporter and the importer. It conforms in all aspects to the agreement between the importer and the exporter. It is similar to pro forma invoice or an ordinary sales invoice. Any visible corrections or changes made in the commercial invoice must be initialed. In the L/C payment method, the description of the goods in the commercial invoice must correspond with the description in the L/C. Transaction value of the products can be found in the commercial invoice.

Customs Invoice: In some countries, mainly those in the British Commonwealth, the commercial invoice must be prepared in a special form prescribed by their customs authorities. They are then known as customs invoices.

Consular Invoice: (not required by all countries) is sometimes required by countries as a means of monitoring imports. Governments can use the consular invoice to monitor prices of imports. It helps the importer to get goods cleared through customs without any undue delay. This invoice requires a detailed description of the goods and has spaces for showing marks, numbers, weight, value of the goods, their origin, and declaration about the accuracy of the contents of the invoice. It must be totally error-free. It is the most difficult document of all and must be prepared with great care.

Forms are purchased from the Consulate of the importing country. These must then be legalized by the Consul. Other documents such as the commercial invoice usually have to be presented to the Consul at the time the consular invoice is validated.

Certificate of Value: Values shown in an invoice often have to be confirmed by a certificate of value signed by the exporter, stating that the invoice contains a true and full statement of the prices paid for the goods and that there is no other understanding between the exporter and the importer about the purchase price. Such a declaration is usually also included in the consular invoice.

Packing List: is an extension of the commercial invoice. It looks like a commercial invoice with additional information such as details of the merchandise, measurements or weight of the cargo, details of goods in each package, cartons and containers, packing, and package numbers. However, it does not indicate the unit price and the value of the goods.

The exporter or his/her agent, the customs broker or the freight forwarder, reserves the shipping space based on the gross weight or the measurement shown in the packing list. Customs uses the packing list as a check-list to verify the outgoing cargo (in case of exporting) and the incoming cargo (in case of importing). The importer uses the packing list to inventory the incoming consignment.

Certain importing countries may require that the commercial invoice and the packing list be translated to the language of the importing country, for example, translation to Russian is needed for shipment to Russia. Some counties use bilingual commercial invoice with both English and local official language. Though, the commercial invoice and packing list need not be signed, unless otherwise stipulated in the L/C, in practice, the original and the copy of the commercial invoice and packing list are often signed.

Export License/ Import License: The export license is a document issued by a national government authorizing the exportation of certain goods from its territory. Similarly the import license is a document issued by a national government authorizing the importation of certain goods into its territory. Quota are administered by licensing. Without license, some goods cannot be traded.

Export declaration/ Import declaration form: All goods meant for import and export are required to be declared in writing in the respective forms. Declaration forms must be filled in detail including providing true information regarding the number, description of packages, value, weight, quantity and type of goods. The origin of the goods and final destination of goods are also needed to be informed. Sample declaration forms can be seen in the Appendix.

Dock Receipt/ Mate Receipt: The document signed by the officer of the vessel (usually by the receiving clerk at the container terminal or dock) to acknowledge that goods have been onboard for shipment. It contains the name of the vessel, shipping line, port of loading, port of discharge, shipping marks and numbers, packing details, description of goods, gross weight, container number, and seal number. It is not a document of title and is issued as an interim measure before a proper bill of lading is issued. Dock receipt transfers the accountability for the safe custody of the cargo from the shipper to the carrier, and serves as the basis for preparing the bill of lading. If a dock receipt is clean, the bill of lading (B/L) issued in due course will be clean.

Bills of Lading (B/L): The bill of lading (in ocean transport), waybill or consignment note (in air, road, rail or sea transport), and receipt (in postal or courier delivery) are collectively known as the transport documents. The B/L serves as
   - a receipt for goods,
   - an evidence of the contract of carriage, and
   - a document of title to the goods.

The carrier issues the B/L according to the information in a dock receipt. The B/L must indicate that the goods have been loaded on board or shipped on a named vessel, and it must be signed or authenticated by the carrier or the master, or the agent on behalf of the carrier or the master.
The B/L should indicate the name of the carrier and signed by the carrier, master or named agent, that goods have been dispatched, taken in charge or shipped on board at the place stated in the letter of credit. The BL should indicate freight pre-paid or freight to collect. The B/L contains the following information:

- Name of the shipping company and the address
- Freight details and name of the vessel
- Consignee's name and address
- Port of loading and port of discharge
- Shipping marks and particulars
- Number of packages shipped on board
- Marking and description of packages
- Gross weight and net weight
- Date of issuance
- Signature (shipping company's agent, carrier's master)

The number of original bills of lading B/L may be expressed as 3/3 (read as 'three of three') or 2/2 (read as 'two of two'). The originals are marked as "original" on their face and all have equal value, that is, all have the same validity. When one of the originals is being surrendered to the carrier, the others become invalid.

Air Waybill is a contract made when the merchandise are carried by air. However, an air waybill is not a negotiable document; it cannot be endorsed. The air waybill is both a receipt for the goods and a contract of carriage. The Air Way Bill should indicate freight pre-paid or freight to collect. Other charges related to shipment are also mentioned. The air Waybill can be divided into 2 types:-
- Master Air Waybill (MAWB)- by the airlines themselves
- House Air Waybill (HAWB) – by the forwarder

When sending cargo by road or rail, the **road waybill** (**road consignment note**) or the **rail waybill** (**rail consignment note**) is issued by the carrier. It serves as a receipt for goods and an evidence of the contract of carriage, but it is not a document of title to the goods.

The **postal receipt, parcel post receipt** and the **courier's receipt** by a courier (or expedited delivery service) are also served as bill of lading as a contract and a receipt.

Types of Bills of Lading

Clean Bill of Lading: The clean bill of lading bears an indication that the goods were received in accordance with the description of the goods without damages, or irregularities. The clean B/L is acceptable to banks for financial settlement of the goods.

Foul Bill of Lading: The foul bill of lading so called unclean bill of lading, dirty bill of lading, is the opposite of the clean bill of lading. It bears an indication that the goods were received with damages, irregularities or short shipment, usually the words "unclean on board" or the like are indicated on the B/L, for example, "insufficient packing", "missing safety seal" and "one carton short". The foul B/L cannot be used to negotiate for payments.

Received Bill of Lading: The received bill of lading does not prove that the goods have been shipped. It only acknowledges that the goods have been received by the carrier for shipment. Therefore, the goods could be in the dock or warehouse.

On Board Bill of Lading: The on board bill of lading, shipped bill of lading, proves that the goods have been shipped inside the carrier, as evidenced by the pre-printed wording or the on board notation (e.g. "on board", "laden on board" or "shipped on board") on the bill of lading.

Straight Bill of Lading: In a straight bill of lading which is also called non-negotiable bill of lading, the title to the goods is conferred directly to a party named in the letter of credit (usually the importer's name), as such the title to the goods is not transferable to another party by endorsement. In other words, the bill of lading is not negotiable. A shipment is consigned to a specific party, usually the importer. Non-negotiable B/L is used where the goods have been paid for or do not require payment (such as donations or gifts). Under this B/L, the consignee does not need an actual B/L to receive the shipment; the shipping company will deliver the shipment to its consignee on presentation of an adequate identification. It is also called consignment bill of lading.

It serves as a receipt for the goods and as an evidence of contract of carriage but is not a document of title. It can be an advantage in that an original is not required to take the delivery of goods. This is useful whenever it is likely that the goods arrive at the port of destination before the relevant document which is common occurrence in international trade, especially on short ocean routes.

Order Bill of Lading: In an order bill of lading which is also called the negotiable bill of lading, is written (drawn) 'To order' of the consignee and is therefore negotiable. The title to the goods is transferable to another party by signature (endorsement), usually on the reverse (back) of the bill of lading. If the endorsement of B/L is required in the L/C, all the originals must be endorsed.

The purpose of an order bill of lading is to protect the interest of the shipper or the named party regarding the title to the goods. The order B/L is usually used when goods have not been paid.

Certificate of Insurance: is of paramount importance in providing insurance cover against possible loss or damage to the specified merchandise during shipment. This insurance policy certificate indicates the type and the amount of coverage.

Rules of Origin Certificate: Rules of origin (ROO) are international rules for determining the 'nationality' of the goods. There are two different types of rules of origin certificate; ordinary certificate of origin and preferential certificate of origin. The ordinary certificate of origin certifies that the products exported are wholly obtained or produced or manufactured in the exporting country.

The preferential certificate of origin is used in claiming preferential tariff under free trade agreements. When goods are presented to customs for clearance purpose at the time of importation, the preferential certificate of origin accompanies the goods and empowers the authorities to permit the preferential import duties. However, rules of origin have multiple standards, and the standards used differ by Free Trade Agreement (FTA). The ROO are important in that they have an impact on procurement strategies of MNEs. In ASEAN, a local content of 40% is required to certify ASEAN nationality of goods. The time consuming and laborious task of acquiring certificate of origin constitutes a cost for companies. ASEAN countries are working on a self-certification scheme for the declaration of origin. This will provide certified economic operators to self-certify the originating status of goods in place of the existing system of presenting certificate of origins issued by government authorities (Sundram, May 2010). Originally, the certificate of origin for ASEAN Common Effective Preferential Tariff is form D which is now replaced by ATIGA form D. The following forms are used in different preferential tariff scheme under the ASEAN free trade agreements.

- Form E (ASEAN– China Free Trade Area)
- Form AK (ASEAN-Korea Free Trade Area)
- Form AANZ (ASEAN-Australia-New Zealand Free Trade Area)
- Form AJ (ASEAN-Japan Free Trade Area)
- ASEAN-India Free Trade Area

Form A (GSP) is used for goods exported under the GSP scheme. The ATIGA form D and the GSP form A can be seen in the Appendix.

Inspection Certificate: The customer sometimes demands a certificate of inspection to ensure the goods meet a certain standard. Consumers have the right to choose and buy safe product. Quality control is very important and different countries have different standards of quality control. For example, exporting fresh fruits to the European Union would need to cut a fruit to check the quality of the fruit inside while the Japanese would check from the outmost shell. However, there are also markets demanding a large amount of products with lower quality checks such as some developing countries and the least developed countries' market.

The attestation is usually performed by a government agency or by an independent testing organization. The exporter must arrange beforehand with the customer regarding who is to carry out such an inspection and who is to pay for it. The followings are some more information on certain inspection certificates.

Certificate of Analysis (CoA): certifies the quality and purity of the products being exported. It certifies that the products adhered to product specification and are manufactured and tested according to the testing organization standards.

Photo Sanitary Certificate:, is the certificate of Plant Protection and Quarantine (PPQ) in line with the FAO International Convention. The purpose of the photo sanitary certificate is to expedite the entry of plants or plant products into a foreign country. This certificate certifies to a foreign country that the plants or plant products described were inspected by the government and are free from quarantined pests and other injurious pests of specific concern to the importing country. This certificate is completed by the Thai Animal and Plant Health Inspection Service, Department of Agriculture, Bangkok, Thailand. Importation of plans and raw plants produce to Thailand, must accompanied a photo sanitary certificate and certification of non-genetically modified plants.

Certificate of Fumigation **(Certificate of Vaccination)**: is a pest control certificate which is used to prevent foreign pests from entering the country through imported products and through wooden packing materials. It is needed that the imported goods are fumigated and certified pest free by the Animal and Plant Health Inspection Service and Plant Protection and Quarantine (PPQ).

Certificate of Analysis for Food Contact Materials certifies the quality and the safety in food contact materials. This is to solve the problem of contamination of food contact materials. In Thailand the certificate can be obtained from the Department of Science Service, Ministry of Science, Thailand (The Nation, 2010b).

Letter of Credit (UPC, 2006): the documentary letter of credit, is a payment guarantee to the beneficiary (the exporter) by the issuing bank (the importer's bank). By issuing L/C, L/C becomes a separate contract between the issuing bank and the beneficiary that bank guarantees to pay or accept to pay the draft (bill of exchange) drawn by the beneficiary against stipulated document(s), provided that the terms and conditions of the documentary credit are fully complied with. The types of letter of credit are as follows:

> **Confirmed letter of credit:** A L/C opened by an issuing bank whose authenticity has been confirmed by the advising bank (usually the exporter's bank) and where the advising bank has added its own guarantee to the credit. The words "we confirm the credit and hereby

undertake ..." or "we add our confirmation to this credit and hereby undertake ..." are included in the L/C.

An exporter whose method of payment is a confirmed L/C is assured of payment even if the issuing bank defaults on payments. The confirmed L/C is particularly important for buyers in a country which is economically or politically unstable. In a confirmed L/C, the exporter or the importer pays an extra charge called the confirmation fee, which may vary from bank to bank within a country. The fee usually is added to the exporter's account.

An **irrevocable letter of credit** cannot be amended or cancelled without the consent of the issuing bank, the confirming bank, if any, and the beneficiary. The payment is guaranteed by the bank if the credit terms and conditions are fully met by the beneficiary. The words "irrevocable documentary credit" or "irrevocable credit" may be indicated in the L/C.

A **revocable letter of credit** can be amended or cancelled by the issuing bank at any time without the consent of the beneficiary, often at the request and on the instructions of the applicant. There is no security of payment in a revocable L/C. The words "this credit is subject to cancellation without notice", "revocable documentary credit" or "revocable credit" usually is indicated in the L/C. It is rarely seen these days in international trade.

Revolving letter of credit: When a L/C is specifically designated "revolving letter of credit", the amount involved when utilized is reinstated, that is, the amount becomes available again without issuing another L/C and usually under the same terms and conditions. The revolving L/C may be used in shipments of a wide range of goods to a buyer within a period of time (usually several months to one year).

Bill of Exchange (draft): is a written order usually by the exporter (drawer) to the importer (drawee) to pay on demand or at a fixed future time a certain sum of money. There are two types of bill of exchange: sight draft and time draft (usance draft).

  Sight draft: Upon presentation of the draft, the drawee has to make the payment immediately. Without making the payment, the documents including B/L will not be released and the buyer cannot take the delivery of the goods. The corresponding terms of payment is referred to as Delivery against Payment (D/P).

  Time draft: When the exporter gives trade credit to the importer, then the exporter draws the time draft. A draft may be drawn according to the trade credit period which is 30 days, 60 days, etc., after it is presented to the drawee (importer) or after the date of shipment. Time draft is accepted for the payment by the issuing bank. The bank accepts to pay by stamping or writing the word "accepted" on the face of the draft. On the due date, the importer makes the payment to the bank. Then the importer's bank forwards the payments to the exporter's bank or to the exporter's account. The corresponding terms of payment is referred to as Delivery against Acceptance (D/P).

Ship arrives before Bill of Lading

  In cases involving the documentary L/C payment terms, the ship often arrives at the port of discharge before the buyer has received the B/L entitling him to take possession of the goods. The ship's master accepts to hand over the goods to the buyer (despite the absence of bill of lading) against security provided by a bank guarantee or a letter of indemnity (LOI).

Figure 6.2 exhibits the documents prepared by the exporters and the importers.

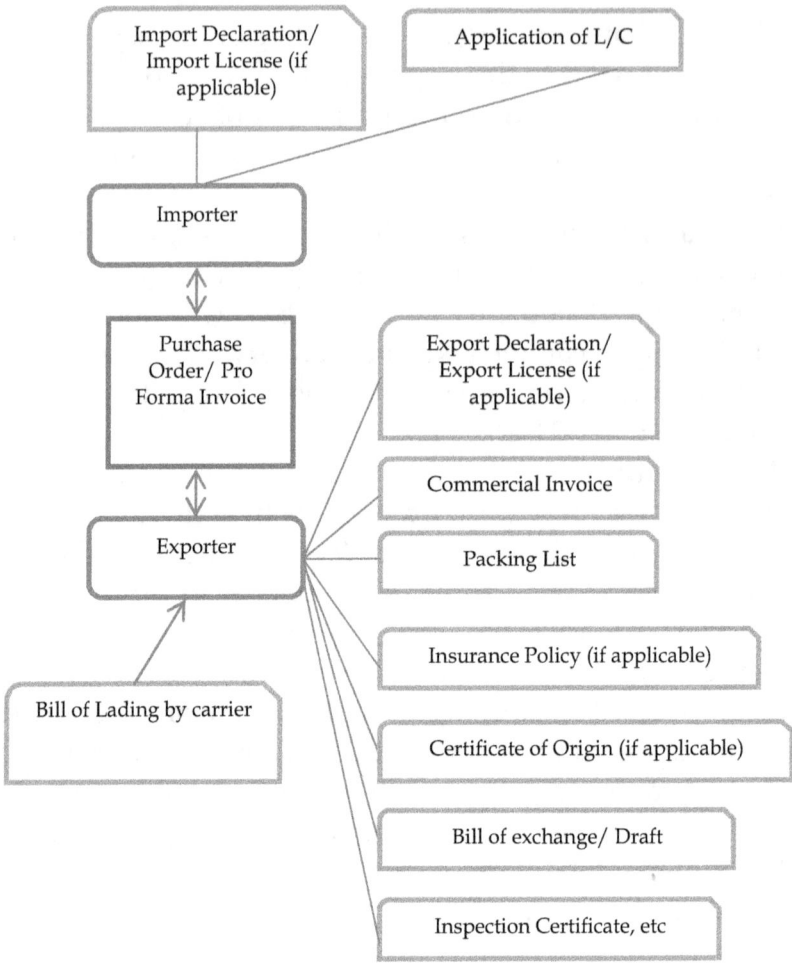

Figure 6.2 Export Import documentation
Source: Author

Reference
- UPC. (2006). UPC 600.

7 International Terms of Payments

Concern about mistrust across international borders is natural. Exporters expect to get paid on time or minimize the risk of nonpayment once the goods have been shipped. On the other hand, importers expect to get goods on time and that goods are exactly what they ordered. Methods of payment help minimizing some of the commercial risks[17] Frequently used payment terms in international trade are

1. Open Account
2. Cash in Advance
3. Collection
    a. Documents against Payment (D/P)
    b. Documents against Acceptance (D/A)
4. Consignment
5. Documentary Letter of Credit (L/C)
    a. Documentary Collection under Sight Draft
    b. Documentary Collection under Time Draft

1. Open Account: Under open account importer gets the goods first and pays later. Open account is sometimes called sales on credit. When importer pays, importer can pay in various ways such as by a cashier cheque, international money order, bank transfer or even by credit card. Open account is advantageous for importer as there is no need to pay for the goods until they have been received and inspected. An importer may even be able to sell the goods and use the proceeds to pay the exporter's commercial invoice when it is due. Some multinational firms make purchase only on open

---

[17] Commercial risk is the default risk either by the exporter or the importer. Risks are of not sending the goods after getting the payment by the exporter or not paying after receiving the goods by the buyer.

account so that they can save the cost of opening a L/C. However, there are risks regarding open account sale. Exporter who makes sales on open account terms should thoroughly examine the political, economic and commercial risk of the transaction.

However, majority of trade, in terms of value, is between affiliated companies or large firms who know and trust each other. A small importer is unlikely to get open account from foreign supplier. Steady purchase and reliable performance will make buying with open account in the future. Figure 7.1 exhibits the open account procedure.

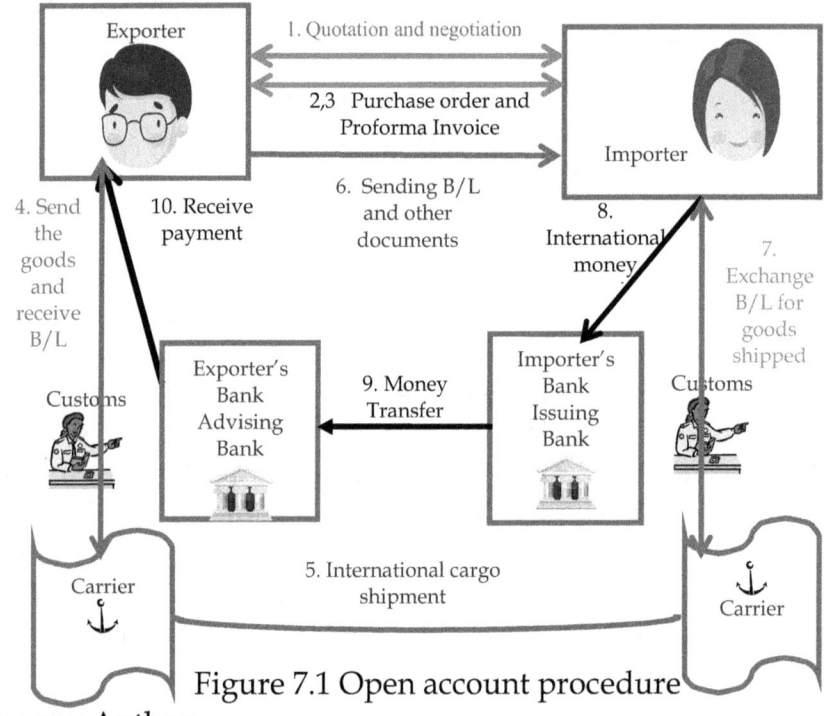

Figure 7.1 Open account procedure

Source: Author

2. **Cash in Advance**: Payment on open account is used when the trading partners have the utmost confidence in each other. At the other extreme, when the exporter has serious doubt about the credit worthiness of the importer (or

economic and political stability of the importing country), the exporter may demand cash in advance. The exporter takes no risks, however, the importer has high risks. If advance payments are made at all, they are usually only partial advance payments (e.g., 20-30%). The buyer can make an advance payment to the seller (other than cash) by bank draft or Telegraphic/Transfer (T/T).

Small transactions such as buying a book, small computer parts, etc usually involve with cash in advance payment. Many exporters who sell through the e-commerce route accept credit card payments. Importers from certain developing countries also find it necessary to pay in advance in order to obtain high-demand goods from developed countries. A variation on cash in advance is "red clause letter of credit" which is discussed under the L/C payment term. Figure 7.2 exhibits the cash in advance procedure.

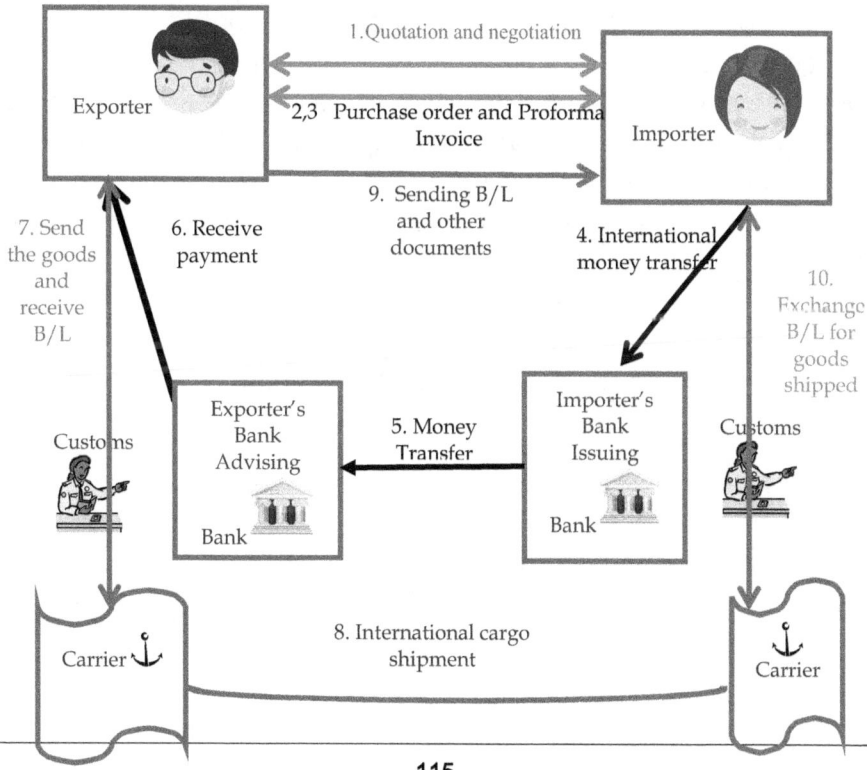

Figure 7.2 Cash in advance procedure
Source: Author

3. Collection: Collection is basically an open account payment made via bill of exchange. It goes through banking channels but banks do not guarantee for payment like under L/C. Documentary collection allows the exporter to retain control of the goods until payment (assurance of payment) is received. Generally the exporter ships the goods and then assembles the relevant documents (commercial invoice, B/L, etc) then turns them over along with a draft (B/E) to a bank acting as a collecting agent for the exporter. The bank will only release the B/L to the importer if the importer pays against the draft (D/P, cash against documents) or accepts the obligation to do so at a future time (D/A, document against acceptance).

For the exporter, the advantage is that documentary collection is easy, inexpensive, and exporter retains control over the goods until the payment or assurance of payment is received. However, the disadvantage is that the importer will not accept the goods shipped.

For the importer, there is no obligation to pay before having had an opportunity to inspect the documents and the goods. The risk for the importer under documentary collection is that the goods shipped might not be as indicated on the invoice and B/L. Typical collection procedures are shown in Figure 7.3.

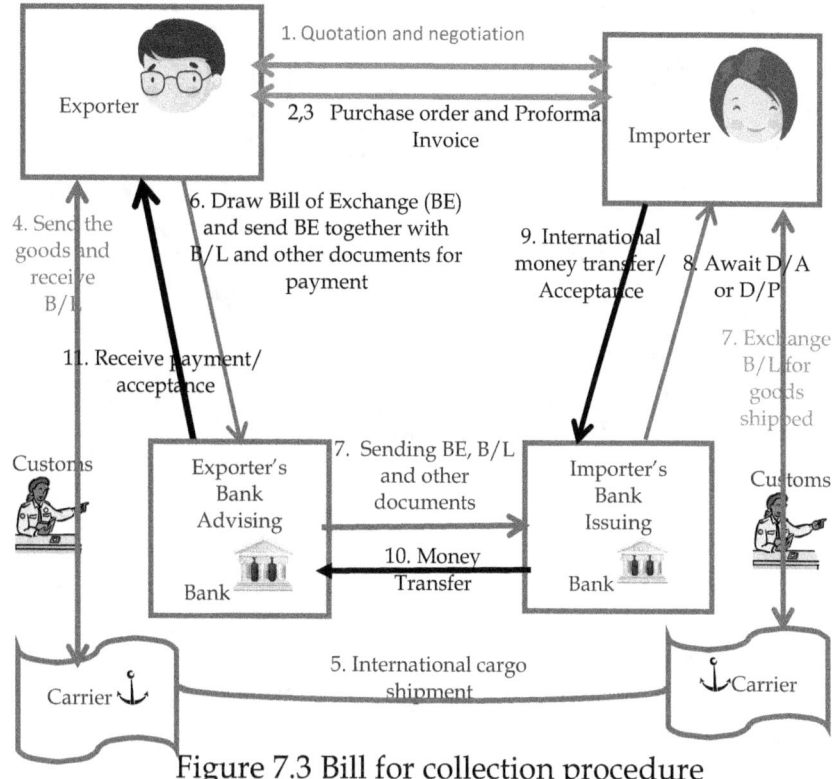

Figure 7.3 Bill for collection procedure

Source: Author

4. Consignment: Consignment is basically an open account payment but then the difference is in consignment the seller is paid only when goods are sold in foreign markets. There might be goods return if goods are unsold. The title of the goods is still with the exporter. This method is too risky for the exporter since no money is tied up in the inventory for the importer. Therefore there is no sales effort by the importer. Figure 7.4 exhibits the typical consignment procedure.

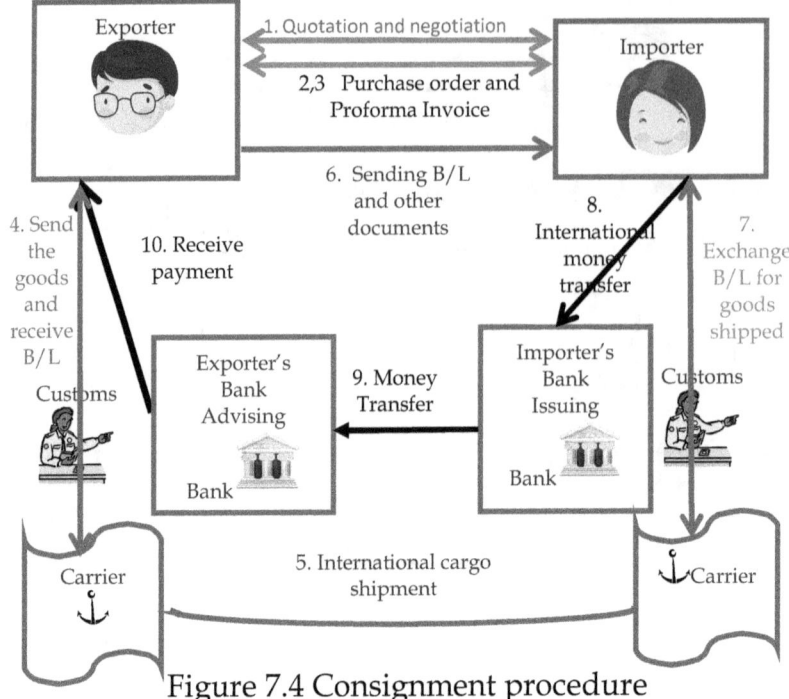

Figure 7.4 Consignment procedure

Source: Author

5. Documentary Letter of Credit (L/C) (UPC, 2006): is most often used when initiating business with a new account, or when a check of the importer's credit reveals that it would be unwise to make shipment on a less secure basis or when large purchases are requested by an unknown buyer. By issuing letter of credit, the bank adds its own liability for the payment on behalf of the importer. For that guarantee, the importer might have to put certain assets as collateral at the bank.

Banks charge a fee for opening the L/C which is based on a percentage of the amount of credit/payment. The exporter usually expects the importer to bear the charges for the L/C but some buyers may not agree to this additional cost. In such cases, the exporter has to either absorb the charges for the L/C or risk losing potential sales.

Payment under an L/C is based on documents not on the physical goods. Under the L/C, the bank, usually the issuing bank (importer's bank) guarantees for payments if documents forwarded from the exporter meet the conditions stipulated in the letter of credit. The bank is not liable for checking physical conditions of the goods.

A credit may be either revocable or irrevocable. The credit, therefore, should clearly indicate whether it is revocable or irrevocable. In the absence of such indication, the credit shall be deemed to be irrevocable.

The credit will call for sight payment or deferred payment. If the credit calls for sight payment, the bank will honor the draft at sight provided that the documents forwarded from the exporter meet the conditions stipulated in the letter of credit. If the credit calls for deferred payment, upon presentation of the documents, the bank will accept to make payment on the maturity date(s) specified on the L/C provided that all the L/C stipulated conditions are met.

A modification made to a L/C after it has been issued is called an amendment. If amendment is needed, the bank charges additional fees for the service.

Usually the following documents are needed under the L/C:

- Draft or Bill of Exchange
- Commercial Invoice,
- Packing List,
- Bill of Lading
- Certificate of Origin,
- Insurance policy(if any)
- Certificate of Health, Certificate of Analysis, Certificate of Inspection, etc.

The documentary L/C procedures are shown in Figure 7.5.

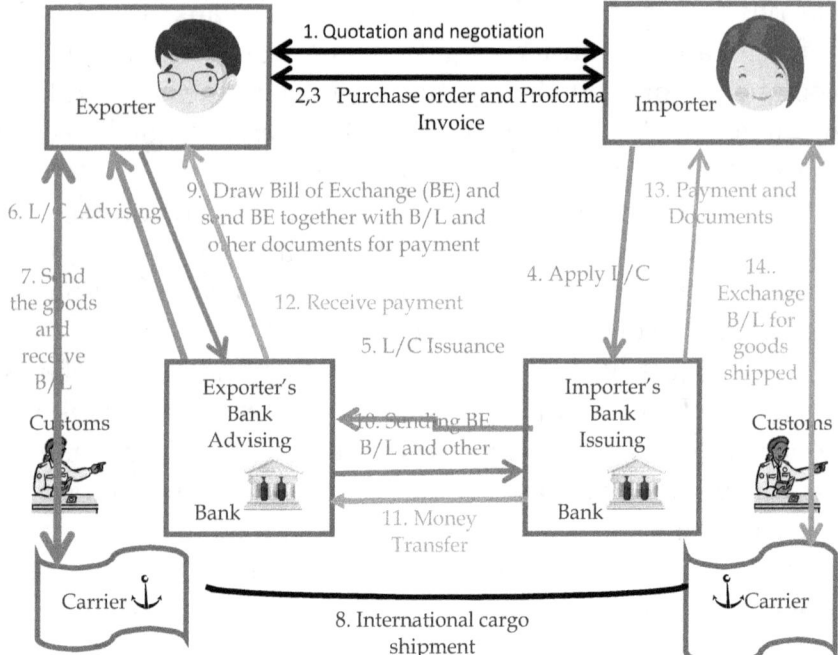

Figure 7.5 Documentary letter of credit procedure
Source: Author

Special Types of Documentary Credit

Red Clause Credit: Importer allows the issuing bank to make pre-shipment advances to the exporter at the risk and expenses of the applicant (importer). The clauses specifying a red clause credit were usually printed or typed in red ink. Under the red clause L/C, the bank will honor the exporter up to the specified percentage of the total credit against production of certain preliminary documents.

If the beneficiary or the seller fails to fulfill his/her obligation, the bank will have the right to demand repayment with interest against the applicant for the credit.

Transferable Credit: is used in "middleman" situations, where an export merchant or agent plays the role of an intermediary between a supplier and the importer. It is normally used when the first beneficiary does not supply the merchandise himself. A credit can be transferred by the original (first) beneficiary to one or more other parties (second beneficiary). The second beneficiary cannot transfer to a third beneficiary.

A credit can be transferred only if it is expressly designated as "transferable" by the issuing bank. Terms such as "divisible", "fractionable", "assignable", and "transmissible" do not render the credit transferable.

At the time of making a request for transfer and prior to transfer of the credit, the first beneficiary must irrevocably instruct the transferring bank whether or not he retains the right to refuse to allow the transferring bank to advise amendments to the second beneficiary. When the transferring bank transfers the credit to the second beneficiary it has to notify the second beneficiary of the first beneficiary's prohibition to advise amendments.

The transferring bank can refuse to transfer the credit until its expenses (i.e. commissions, fees, costs, etc.) are paid; without specific instructions, the first beneficiary is responsible for payment of these expenses. Sample application form of transferable L/C can be seen in the Appendix.

The credit can be transferred only on the terms and conditions specified in the original letter of credit, with the exception of:
- the amount of the credit,
- any unit price stated therein,
- the expiry date,
- the last date for presentation of documents
- the period for shipment, any or all of which may be reduced or curtailed.

The first beneficiary can be named in documents instead of the applicant, unless the credit specifically requires. The first beneficiary has the right to substitute his own invoice(s) (and draft(s)) for those of the second beneficiary/beneficiaries. The right to substitute invoices and drafts enables the first beneficiary to claim his profit, i.e. the difference between the original amount of the credit and the transfer amount. If the first beneficiary fails to supply his invoice and draft the transferring bank is authorized to deliver the documents received under the credit from the second beneficiary to the issuing bank. Thus the first beneficiary loses his chance to protect his sources; however, until the credit expires he retains the right to supply his invoice in exchange for the second beneficiary's invoice.

Back to Back Credit (counter credit): Under back to back credit, the middleman-beneficiary uses the letter of credit as security for a second, separate credit in favor of the ultimate supplier. In other words, the seller as beneficiary of the first credit offers the first L/C as security to the advising bank for the issuance of the second credit. The supplier becomes the beneficiary of the back-to-back credit. The amount of the second credit is less than the original export credit and the difference is the import agent's commission.

A 'back-to-back' arrangement may become necessary where the underlying contracts are on terms that do not match, or where a transferable credit is unable to maintain confidentiality on a particular aspect of the transaction. The need for such a credit may also arise where
a) the ultimate buyer is not ready to open a transferable L/C, or
b) the beneficiary is not ready to disclose to the buyer the source of his supply, and
c) the manufacturer insists on payment against documents or goods but the beneficiary is short of funds.

Stand by Letter of Credit: is served as a security or guarantee rather than as a payment mechanism. Some governments do not allow banks to guarantee for payment, then the stand by letter of credit is used.

Credit Application

While applying for an L/C, the instructions given by the applicant to the issuing bank will cover such items as:
- The full and correct name and address of the beneficiary
- The amount of the credit
- The types of credit whether it is revocable, irrevocable, or irrevocable with the added confirmation of the advising bank
- How the credit is to be available e.g. by payment, by acceptance or negotiation
- The party on whom drafts, if any, are to be drawn and the tenor of such drafts
- A brief description of the goods, including details of quantity and unit price
- Whether freight is to be prepaid or not
- Details of documents required e.g. certificate of analysis
- Place of loading, place of discharging or final destination
- Whether trans-shipment is prohibited
- Whether partial shipments are prohibited
- The latest date of shipment and the date and place of expiry of the credit
- Whether the credit is to be a transferable one
- How the credit is to be advised e.g. by mail, telex or swift

The sample L/C application form can be seen in the Appendix.

Reference
- UPC. (2006). UPC 600.

8 Export Import Financing

International settlement needs trade financing. The main objectives of financing to exporters and importers are as follows. For the exporter, *financing* gives working capital to pay for manufacturing goods, marketing effort, etc. For the importer, *financing* offers the ability to pay for the overseas suppliers and cost of shipment of foreign goods designated or targeted for the home market.

The exporters and importers get export-import financing through
- Commercial banks
- Factors and other private sources of financing and
- Government sources (for example Export Import Bank (EXIM Bank))

Trade Financing by Commercial Banks

Commercial banks offer various types of pre-shipment and post-shipment loans/credit lines to exporters and importers to increase their working capital and liquidity. The followings are offered for the exporters by commercial banks (Bangkok Bank, 2011; Bank of Ayudhya, 2011; Kasikornbank, 2011; Siam Commercial Bank, 2011) .

Pre-shipment financing for exporters: For exporters who want the working capital to procure raw materials for production or to pay for other expenses to produce finished goods, banks provide with pre-shipment financing called packing credit. The offered credit lines are usually divided into 3 categories; packing credit against L/C, packing credit against contract, packing credit against stock.

Packing Credit is the low interest financing system that the EXIM bank gives to the exporter through the commercial banks. Usually the bank gives 80 percent credit of the value in the L/C, contract or stock.

Post-Shipment financing for exporters: Before getting payment from trade partners (importer) or the L/C-issuing bank, exporters can get money instantly when they submit the export bill for collection (B/C) or export bills under L/C to the bank. Export Bill means the bill of exchange or drafts that exporter draws after sending the goods. The bank gives 100 percent credit per value shown in export bills. Interest charges depend on the banks.

Pre-Shipment financing for importers: When initiating a new business, exporter usually asks the bank guarantee before sending the goods to the importer. Bank issues L/C guaranteeing for payment. The issuance of L/C is pre-shipment financing for importer. The L/C details are discussed in the previous chapters.

Post-Shipment financing for importers: There is a service called trust receipt arrangement where the bank pays for imported goods on behalf importer before the bank gets payment from importer. The importers can benefit from trust receipt arrangement as they can use the funds from the pending payment as working capital in their business. The trust receipt interest rate is lower than that of Promissory Note (P/N).

Other Services

Banks also provide other services to facilitate international trade such as, bank guarantee services, import related services and export related services.

Bank guarantee service assures against loss incurred by uncompleted performance under agreement, and helps to ease concerns about contractual defaults. In order to meet various types of trade transactions or contractual obligations, international bank guarantee / standby L/C and international counter guarantee services are offered by banks.

Bank's international bank guarantee/standby L/C_is a bank guarantee in the form of 'guarantee' or 'standby L/C' to a beneficiary in a foreign country by the request of domestic exporter/seller or importer/buyer to undertake the payment or performance liability towards the beneficiary. The bank guarantee can also be used as collateral to obtain loans from other private financial institutions abroad.

International counter guarantee increases the confidence of foreign trade partners. Cooperation between local banks and alliance banks in foreign countries jointly undertake obligation and issue local guarantee/standby L/C directly to trade partners. The beneficiary (foreign partner) can claim directly from their local issuing bank to compensate loss incurred by any default on business agreement/contract.

Import related services
Banks provide professional handling of all import related services such as
- Import L/C issuance
- Import domestic L/C issuance
- Import payment under B/C
- Shipping guarantee issuance and delivery order endorsement
- Forward exchange sold

Import L/C Issuance: By issuing a L/C, the bank guarantees to pay for goods or services per the request of the applicant (importer) to the exporter via the exporter's advising bank. The bank will pay the exporter if he fulfills all terms and conditions specified in the L/C.

This L/C issuance service also has other related services such as L/C amendment or cancellation. With irrevocable L/C, L/C amendment and cancellation can take effect only when the beneficiaries mentioned in the L/C, the issuing bank and confirming bank (if any) have all given their consent. All L/Cs must be in accordance with the revised Uniform Customs and Practices for Documentary Credits 2007 (UPC 600) of the International Chamber of Commerce (ICC).

Import Domestic L/C (DL/C) Issuance: By issuing DL/C, the bank facilitates domestic buyers wishing to order goods from domestic sellers. The features and procedure of DL/C are the same as in the foreign L/C.

Import Payment Under B/C: The bank acts as a mediator in collecting payment for goods and services from domestic buyers or importers to pay oversea sellers. The payment of this import payment under bills for collection has 3 conditions as follows:
   (1) Deliver Document against Payment (D/P): The bank will release the document to the buyer when the buyer has fully paid the bank.
   (2) Deliver Document against Acceptance (D/A): The Bank will submit the document to the buyer after having accepted the D/A to the bank. This guarantees the repayment to the bank in the future under agreement.
   (3) Deliver Document under other Terms and Conditions: The bank will submit the document to the buyer under other terms and conditions. For instance, the document will be submitted to the buyer against a Letter of Undertaking or Letter of Indemnity to pay in the future date, etc.

Shipping Guarantee Issuance and Delivery Order Endorsement: The bank issues a shipping guarantee to a sea freight company or its representative (it is called delivery order endorsement if air freight is used) to allow the importer to receive goods at the port without the original marine B/L or Air Waybill. When imported goods arrive before the bank receives the shipping documents, with shipping guarantee or delivery order endorsement, the importer can proceed customs clearance without the original marine B/L or Air Waybill.

Forward Exchange Sold: is a service available to importers to mitigate foreign exchange volatility risk. By entering into a forward exchange sold contract, the importer fixes the exchange rate in advance of the delivery date.

Export related services
Banks provide professional handling of all export related services such as
- Export L/C advising
- L/C confirmation
- L/C transfer
- Assignment of proceeds under export L/C
- Export collection under L/C
- Export collection under B/C
- Forward Exchange Bought

Export L/C Advising: The bank advises the exporters that an L/C has been opened in the exporter's name once the bank has received SWIFT message from the issuing bank abroad.

L/C Confirmation: For exporters who need more security in receiving payment under the L/C, the bank can serve with the L/C confirmation service. By confirming L/C, the bank is liable for payments drawn under the credit provided that all L/C stipulated terms are met. The bank's adding confirmation will be terminated if the beneficiary fails to comply with all terms and conditions specified in the L/C.

L/C Transfer: It is a beneficial service for the exporter acting as a middleman who is the first beneficiary of the L/C. The bank will transfer the rights and benefits of the first beneficiary under the terms and conditions of a transferable L/C to a secondary beneficiary (supplier or manufacturer), as requested by the first beneficiary of the L/C. However, the L/C shall not be transferred unless it indicates the transferable condition.

Assignment of Proceeds under Export L/C: The exporter who acts either as a middleman to purchase goods from domestic manufacturers, or as a manufacturer who needs sourcing goods from other manufacturers, the bank can act as a coordinator in assigning the proceeds under the export L/C requested by the beneficiary in the L/C to an assignee. The proceeds mean payments that exporter receive from importer. This service makes it easier for the exporter to make payments to manufacturers after receiving payment under the export L/C collection. The assignment of proceeds must take place domestically. The proceeds can be allocated to as many assignees as required.

Export Collection under L/C: When traders use L/C as payment method, the bank acts as the nominated bank authorized by the L/C issuing bank to collect payment from the L/C issuing bank by sending the documents for collection under the L/C provided that all terms and conditions have been complied with the L/C.

Export Collection under B/C: When traders use collection as international payment, the bank acts as the remitting bank responsible for sending financial and commercial documents submitted by the seller for collection of payments from the buyer via the collecting bank under the terms and conditions agreed between the buyer and the seller. Every party in the documents under B/C has to follow the ICC Uniform Rules for Collection (URC522). There are three types of collection under B/C, which are:

1. Document against Payment (D/P)

   The buyer is required to make full payment to his bank before receiving the documents. If the draft drawn is sight draft, D/P shall be made.

2. Document against Acceptance (D/A)

   Buyers receive documents from the bank to receive goods after they have accepted the terms of payment as per details specified in the time draft.

3. Document against Other Undertaking

   The buyer is required to present or accept any form of undertaking before receiving the document from his bank.

Forward Exchange Bought: is a service available to exporters to mitigate foreign exchange volatility risk by entering into a forward exchange bought contract. With forward contract, the exporter fixes the exchange rate in advance of the delivery date.

Trade Financing by Factor

A factor is a bank or a specialized financial firm that performs financing through the purchase of invoices or accounts receivable.

Export factoring is offered under an agreement between the factor and exporter, in which the factor purchases the exporter's short-term foreign accounts receivable for cash at a discount from the face value, normally without recourse, and assumes the risk on the ability of the foreign buyer to pay, and handles collections on the receivables.

Trade Financing by Government Sources

There are many trade and investment financing facilities provided by the EXIM bank of Thailand (EXIM Thailand, 2011) such as

- **working capital loans** to the exporters to meet their financial needs.
- **Export credit insurance** to covers both commercial risk and political risk for the exporters.
- **Buyer/Bank risk assessment report** to check the credit information of each buyer/issuing bank.
- **Buyer's credit** of medium- to long-term credit facility provided to overseas buyers to promote the import of goods and/or services from the country.
- **Term loans** to support exporters who need credits for various purposes.
- **Export advisory service and**
- **Many others**

For detail information, visit the EXIM bank of Thailand at **www.exim.go.th**.

Reference

- Bangkok Bank. (2011). Trade Service. from http://www.bangkokbank.com/Bangkok%20Bank/Busin ess%20Banking/Pages/default.aspx
- Bank of Ayudhya. (2011). Trade Services. from http://www.krungsri.com/en/corporate-financial-listing.aspx?pid=63
- EXIM Thailand. (2011). from www.exim.go.th
- Kasikornbank. (2011). International Trade. from http://www.kasikornbank.com/EN/Business/Internatio nalTrade/Pages/InternationalTrade.aspx

- Siam Commercial Bank. (2011). Business Banking. from
  http://www.scb.co.th/en/business-banking#
- UPC. (2006). UPC 600.

9 Global Transportation

Not all products are produced and consumed in the same location; they are needed to be moved from the place of origin to the others. The movement of goods from one place to another place requires proper transportation platform. Transportation and logistics infrastructure is a critical issue for exporters and importers as well as governments seeking to attract new industries or retain existing firms. While sending goods globally, choice of global transportation mode depends on the mode availability, transportation infrastructure and port facility of the particular country as well as service components of particular mode.

Global transportation is facilitated by road, rail, sea (ocean), air and pipeline. Mode availability varies from country to country. Certain countries such as the Laos People's Democratic Republic, the Kingdom of Bhutan and many countries in Africa are landlocked and thus these countries are inaccessible by deep-sea ocean vessels. Therefore, goods intended for/from those landlocked countries must be trans-shipped in another country or countries by means of truck and/or rail and/or inland waterway (i.e., river, canal or lake) transports.

In addition to mode availability, logistic infrastructure is another important issue. Logistic infrastructure among 10 ASEAN counties varies. Some countries have well- connected roads, however, the conditions of the roads are very poor. Consequently, it takes a long time to transport the goods from one place to another place. The following table 9.1 compares the logistic infrastructure among ten ASEAN countries.

Thus selection of international transportation mode depends on mode availability and logistic infrastructure of the country. In addition, the nature of the product to be sent and

Table 9.1 Table of Comparison: Logistics Infrastructure of Countries in ASEAN

	Sea Port	Airport	Railway	Road
Cambodia	Poor	Fair	Poor	Poor
Indonesia	Poor	Fair	Good	Fair
Laos	Not applicable	Poor	Not applicable	Fair
Malaysia	Good	Good	Good	Good
Philippines	Fair	Fair	Poor	Fair
Singapore	Good	Good	Good	Good
Thailand	Good	Good	Good	Good
Vietnam	Fair	Fair	Fair	Fair
Burma	Poor	Poor	Poor	Fair

Source: http://www.business-in-asia.com/infrastructure_ASEAN.html

the logistic distance between point of origin and destination also determine the mode selection. Thus, the service components of the particular mode are needed to be considered. The logistic service components are:

1. **Transit time:** is the time needed to move the goods from one place to another place. It affects the level of inventory (buffer stock) held by both the shipper and receiver and the cost of holding inventory. The longer the transit time the greater the potential cost of stock outs as well. Perishable products need a shorter transit time.

2. **Cost:** depends on the value of the service each mode offers to the shipper. High-priced items can absorb transportation costs more easily than low-priced items.

3. **Reliability:** refers to the consistency of transit time.

4. **Accessibility:** is the ability of the transportation provider to move the freight between origin and destination. The inability of a carrier to provide direct service between an

origin and destination results in added costs and transit time for the shipper.

5. **Capability:** is the ability of the carrier to provide the special service demanded by the shipper. Some shippers have unique demands for equipment, facilities and communication. For example, some products require temperature control; some shippers need consolidation and break bulk service; some transportation modes can handle large or heavy cargos. In the past, transportation of perishable products is not possible with road transportation even for cross border shipments. With the technology innovation, nowadays trailers with high power engines which can accommodate refrigerated cargos, are capable of carrying perishable cargos.

6. **Security:** is concerned with safety of the goods in transit.

7. **Non-economic factors:** Government preferential policies (the use of national carrier though a more economical alternative exists)

The following table 9.2 compares the service components of road, rail, water, air and pipeline transportation.

Table 9.2 Service components of road, rail, water, air and pipeline transportation

Service components	Mode of Transportation				
	Road	Rail	Waterway	Air	Pipeline
Transit time (1= fastest)	2	3	5	1	4
Accessibility (1 = best)	1	2	4	3	5
Capability[1] (1=best)	3	2	1	4	5
Cost (1= highest)	2	3	5	1	4

Source: author (adopted from Ranald, Ballou, Business Logistic management 4th ed., p. 146)

The inability of a carrier to provide direct service requires additional transportation by truck and rail.

Multimodal Transport also called intermodal transport occurs when two modes or more are used in transportation of goods from origin to destination under a single contract. There are different forms of multimodal transport operation.

Land bridge: is a generic term meaning use of land freight as a means of transport connection: a service in which foreign cargo crosses a country en route to another country (passes overland in a third country). It is a way of transporting cargo from a port or an inland point of origin in the shipper's country to an inland point or a port of final destination in the consignee's country using a combination of usually sea and land, or air and land, or air, land and sea transports, instead of relying fully on journey by water or air. The following Diagram 1 is the example of landbridge which use Vietnam, Cambodia, Thailand and Myanamar's land as bridge in transport connection of South China sea and Andaman Sea.

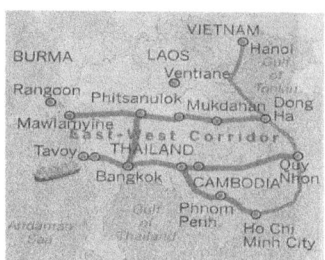

Diagram 9.1 Landbridge in ASEAN
source: The Nation

Mini-land-bridge (mini-bridge): Shipment from a country's port to another country's port with overland journey in the first country. (shipments from port of Seattle (Washington, USA) to the port of Rotterdam (Netherlands) involves the cargo being delivered via rail to (New York, USA) and then to Rotterdam.

Micro-bridge: Shipment from a country's port to another country's inland destination and vice versa. This service provides door to door service rather than port to port transportation.

The advantages of multimodal are that it provides a combined rate including rail and ocean in the freight rate that is lower than the sum of the separate rates. It also reduces the burden of documentation and formalities connected with each segmented transport chain to minimum (UNESCAP, 2011). It also provides faster transit of goods and it is useful for cargos which are semi-sensitive to time and cost.

In the multimodal transportation, the multimodal transport B/L is used. Although the multimodal B/L serves as a receipt for delivery of goods, it is not necessarily evidence that they have been shipped on board an ocean-going vessel. Transport documents covering a multimodal shipment include the B/L, the road waybill, the rail waybill or an inland waterway transport document.

The B/L in multimodal shipment can be a document of title whereas land carriage documents are not documents of title. These documents are issued subject to different liability regime. The multimodal transport B/L is issued subject to the network liability system whereby the existing mandatory rules governing unimodal carriage will apply when the loss or damage to the goods occurs in that particular mode (Cioarec, 2007).

Dry Port is an inland intermodal terminal directly connected by rail or road to one or more container seaports. Dry ports are for transit of goods from one transport mode to another, such as from rail to road. A container freight train runs between the seaport and the dry port. The functions of the dry port includes cargo handling, intermodal or unimodal handling of cargo and containers, and storage of empty or loaded containers. It also includes warehouse logistic functions, custom inspection and clearance functions related to international trade, information technology to facilitate transport, freight forwarding and immigration related service. The Transport Ministry of Thailand plans to increase the number of dry ports to enhance the country's logistic system in preparation of the ASEAN Economic Community in 2015 (Thongrung, 2010) Currently Thailand has only one dry port, the Inland Container Deport in Bangkok's Lat Krabang district (Thongrung, 2010).

Nowadays, concerns over environmental issues become serious. Thus, some shippers switch from inland transportation of containers from trucks to either railways or waterways with relatively shorter distance with low cost and low environmental impact called *Modal Shift Transport*. The Modal Shift transport service reduces transportation cost, stabilizes the lead time and improves corporate brand.

Role of Custom Brokers and Freight Forwarders in International Transport

In practice only the largest exporters try to handle all the shipping and dispatching of their goods overseas themselves. With large quantities of goods to export, they can afford to employ their own export staff.

Small exporters find it easier to use the services of **shipping and forwarding agents,** or *freight forwarders* as they are sometimes called. Once an exporter makes a foreign sale, he/she hires the freight forwarder. The freight forwarders are experts on finding the availability of the different modes of transport for different markets, the optimal logistic cost, and the suitability of each mode. They will get the products from the exporter's factory and transport them to the docks, airport, railway station or road collection points and then overseas. Their job involves booking space, arranging for inland carrier, arranging documentation such as reviewing letter of credit, obtaining export license if necessary, and preparing required shipping documents and necessary storage prior to shipment.

They deal with customs entries and other formalities and they will route the cargo at the lowest custom charges. They may also advise on the degree of packing and labeling, and cargo insurance. The freight forwarder usually charges the exporter percentage of the shipment value, plus a minimum charge depending on the number of services provided. They also receive a brokerage fee from the carrier. However, they do not take title of goods or act as sales representatives in a foreign country. They just render cargo delivery services. They also do freight consolidation.

Freight consolidator is an individual or firm who accepts less than the container load (LCL) shipments from individual shippers and then combines them for delivery to the carrier in full container load (FCL) shipment. Consolidating or grouping together a number of consignments make transportation more economic.

The freight consolidator usually receives the forwarder's charges from the exporter plus a commission from the carrier. The forwarder may buy the shipping space, in a special arrangement with the carrier and resell the space to individual shippers, instead of receiving the commission. In such an agreement, the forwarder functions as an independent distributor or logistical company known as NVOCC (The Non-Vessel-Operating Common Carrier) or NVO (Non-Vessel Owner). A forwarder must issue a B/L to the shipper called House B/L. In doing so the forwarder accepts the responsibility for the shipment, thus he must accept liability for loss and /or damage to a shipment. Figure 9.1 shows the role of the freight forwarder/consolidator.

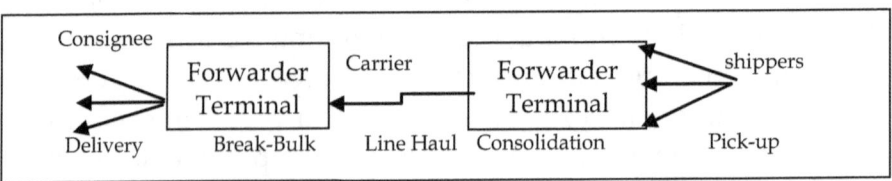

Figure 9.1 Forwarder Operation
Source: Author

Custom broker: is an individual or a company licensed to clear export and import goods through customs. They also render forwarding services as freight forwarders. They provide export related services such as booking of space, providing freight costs, preparation of export documentation and import related services such as advising on the technical requirements of importing, preparing and filing entry documents, obtaining necessary bonds (which is needed to ensure payment of proper amounts of duties, taxes and other charges associated with entry), depositing import duties, securing release of cargo, arranging delivery to the importer's premises or warehouse, and obtaining 'drawback' refund. They charge service fees as a uniform based fees plus a small percentage of the value of shipment.

Packing and Marking for Shipment

Shipping products thousands of miles in undamaged condition needs the package to be protected from breakage caused by rough weather and storms, rough handling, careless storage, dampness caused by heat and humidity of the tropics as well as rainstorms and rough weather at sea and pilferage. Thus the export packing needs to be stronger and heavier than what is used for domestic shipment. To avoid breakage, the goods should not be overpacked. To avoid dampness, waterproof packing is needed. To avoid pilferage, it is better to use strappings and seals and avoid trademarks or content description. Diagram 9.2 shows packaging of printer cartridge.

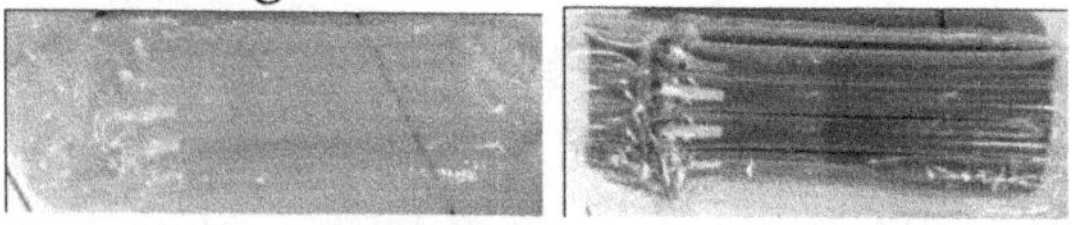

Diagram 9.2 Packaging
Source: Author

Packing for transit has to tradeoff between two considerations. Packing must be strong enough to stand transportation hazards. It must also be as light or compact as possible to keep freight costs low. Rates are usually quoted on weight/measure basis. Boxes that are large in relation to their weight are charged by the amount of space they occupy. Boxes that are heavy in relation to their size are charged according to their weight. It is estimated that 80% of cargo is shipped by volume rather than by weight, so that the saving of a few centimeters on the dimension of each packing case in a large shipment could make a difference in the freight cost. If the shipments are small, they will be sent break bulk or less than container load (LCL) called break bulk packing. It might cost higher than the full container load (FCL).

For further information, visit www.freight-calculator.com. Basically there are three stages in packaging for export; sales packaging, export packaging and outer packaging. The following diagram 9.3 illustrates the stages of packaging.

Packing should meet any specifications laid down in the customer's country and should carry certain markings. The sales packaging of many commodities is subject to detailed labeling as well, and many shipping lines and insurance companies expect goods to be packed according to such requirements.The first marking an exporter must consider for his goods is the *mark of origin*. The mark of origin must be readable, indelible (impossible to remove), and easily seen. The particular way in which the mark is applied depends on the particular country. The exporter should always look into the importing country's marking regulations before packing and marking his goods for export shipment.

Shipping marks such as 'Handle with care', 'Use no hook', 'This way up', 'Sling here', 'Keep away from heat', 'Center of gravity', 'Keep dry' are common. They should be clearly stamped on each case. Diagram 9.4 shows some of the markings. Other markings requested by the buyer are often a distinctive shape with the customer's initials inside them.

Underneath the mark the destination is given as well as the number of cases in the shipment and which case that particular one is of the set. For example, the first case of ten cases would be signified 1/10. The weights and measurements of each case should also be indicated.

Diagram 9.3 Stages of packaging
Source: Author

Diagram 9.4 Marking on export packaging
Source: Author

Labeling: Special rules apply to the labeling of certain products, including prepared foodstuffs, beverages, pharmaceuticals, and toilet preparations. The label should make clear the quantity and quality of the goods. Some certification logo such as HACCP, GMP, Halal, ISO are also printed on the packages. The information on the labels may include name and address of manufacturer, weight or volume of contents, ingredients and other relevant details. Diagram 9.5 shows some of the markings.

Diagram 9.5 Labeling on export packaging
Source: Author

Cargo Unitization

The speed of cargo handling is very important, especially when goods are transferred between different modes of transport for example from ships to road, from road to rail. Cargo unitization allows ships to spend much less time loading and unloading at docks or ports as well as reduces the risks of damage and theft.

Cargo unitization: When several boxes are put together to make one unit, it is called cargo unitization. It is the way small items of cargo are put together and handled as a unit of standard size, usually by using mechanical equipment.

To enhance safety, losses, humidity, damages, fast and convenient transfer from the country of origin to the country of destination, many types of containers are designed to fit special requirements on the merchandise (commodities) shipped. This reduces the amount of labor required to move the goods and speeds up the cargo handling process. Types of cargo unitization include:
- containerization
- palletization
- roll-on, roll-off vessels
- barge-carrying vessels

Containerization: This is the best known kind of cargo unitization, and consists of packing cargoes in standard size containers so that they can be handled quickly and easily by standardized equipment.

Containerization has gained popularity from the 1960s onwards, mainly on the deep-sea trade routes between the industrial countries of North America, Western Europe, Australia and Japan.

Inside a container the goods are almost completely protected from corrosion or pilferage. The possibility of rough handling is reduced and so a lighter packing can be used. This can save the exporter a good deal of money and means that he can quote a lower price to his customer. Port authorities also charge fewer tariffs for containerized cargo for easy handling. Easy handling also reduces warehousing and inventory costs, insurance premium, packing costs, etc. For the ship owners, containerization also provides more cargo carrying capacity and speeds up cargo handling at the port, etc. Containers can be divided into 3 main types:

1.1 General purpose (dry cargo) container
1.2 Specific purpose container
1.3 Specific cargo container

General Purpose Containers are suitable for general merchandise (cargo). It is also known as a dry freight container and it is the most widely used shipping container. It is commonly used for all types of cargo that are not affected by changes in temperature. There are _20'ft (footer) and 40'ft (footer)_ standard containers with the following dimensions.

20'ft (footer) L20' x W8' x H8.6' and
40'ft (footer) L40' x W8' x H8.6'

There are also high cube container- <u>hicube</u> – H 9.5' and <u>half height container</u> H4.25' or 4.3'. Not all shipping companies and sea routes have the hicube. Hicube containers are designed to carry voluminous cargo. Automobiles are also carried using hicube. There are legal limitations to the overall height of a vehicle in certain areas (eg. Tunnel and underpass) and countries. The FCL freight rate of hicube is higher than the standard container. The half high container is designed for heavy loads such as steel rods and ingots which absorb the weight limit in half the normal space. The followings show different types of containers.

Standard container   High Cube container   Half High container

Source: author   source: starwarsblog.starwars.com Source: author   source:mrbox.co.uk

On one side of the container, the following markings can be found; rating, tare mass and payload.

• <u>Rating</u>: the maximum gross mass (weight) : maximum permissible weight of a container plus its contents.

- Tare Mass: the mass (weight) of empty container
- Payload: maximum permitted mass (weight)
- Thus Payload = Rating – Tare Mass

Marking on the wall of the container

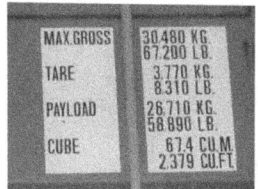

Source: author

For example for 20' Dry Freight Container: L20' x W8' x H8.6'
Rating : 24,000 kgs.
Tare Weight: 1,800 – 2,400 kgs.
Pay Load: 22,100 kgs (24,000 – 2,400).

For 40' Dry Freight Container: L40' x W8' x H8.6'
Rating : 30,480 kgs
Tare Weight: 2,800 – 4,000 kgs.
Pay Load: 26,580 kgs (30,480 – 3,9000)

Specific Purpose Containers
Open Top Container: - is similar to dry cargo container except
that it has no rigid roof, but has a movable or removable
cover. They are used for machinery, sheet glass and other
heavy, bulky or long objects.

Side Open Container: The container can be opened from both
of its side boards or use tarpaulin sheets are used to cover the
container's sides. This is to load cargo with excessive width or
length.
Platform Based Container or Flat Rack: does not have a
superstructure, that is rigid sides walls and load-carrying

structures. Normally, there are lashing devices on the floor of the container and detachable container's boards.

It is designed to accommodate cargoes, such as machinery, vehicles or forestry products, whose overall dimensions exceed those of a general purpose container. It is used for heavy-lifts and over wide cargo.

Open top container   Side open container Flat rack

 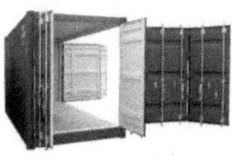 

source: hiwtc.com

Source: http://containerhouse.en.made-in-china.com   source: http://www.shippingcontainers24.com

Specific Cargo Containers

<u>Termal Containers</u>: - are used for cargo that can quickly deteriorate or be destroyed in normal temperature or environment.

Reefer Container: Refrigerated equipment is installed as part of the container to keep the temperature in the container up to the requirement of shippers or liners. A refrigeration unit is connected to the carrying ship's electrical power supply. The ventilation is blown from the back or from the ceiling of the container. The container has the capacity to control the temperature down to a level of –10 degree Fahrenheit or –23 degree Celsius. They are normally for perishable cargoes e.g. fruits, vegetables or frozen food.

Insulated Container: These are normal box containers with insulating material in the walls, top and bottom. As a result, there is minimum temperature fluctuation inside. They are also attached to a separate temperature control device (temperature control containers).

Tank Containers: A limited number of containers are deployed exclusively for the transport of liquors and liquid foods. It consists of a cylindrical tank made of stainless steel surrounded by a framework, which provides the same overall dimensions as those of a standard dry cargo container enabling it to be carried and handled in the same way. Products carried in tank containers range from potable spirits, such as whisky, to hazardous chemicals. Only 20'ft containers are available.

Dry Bulk containers: are used for carriage of dry solids in bulk without packaging, such as grains and dry chemicals.

Livestock containers: are used to carry animals.

Reefer container   Livestock containers

Source: lico.en.hisupplier.com Source: author

Dry bulk container Tank Container

 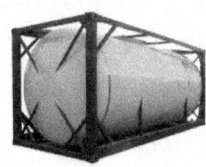

source: www.cimc.com   Source: maritrade.com

Palletization is a simplified version of containerization. When the unit is too large and heavy to handle easily, it is put on the wooden or plastic platforms or pallets. These are of a standard size designed to be picked up and put down quickly and easily by fork lift trucks and other handling equipment.

Cargoes are said to be palletized. It is much more likely to be usable by exporters in developing countries. The standard European pallet is 120cm by 80cm and the units are bound to it by steel bands or tension strapping. The pallet loads of goods are then stacked on top of each other or in racks. This method is the most successful with specially designed equipment and ships, but pallets can be used effectively on ordinary general cargo ships. Ships at sea move in different directions simultaneously, thus they always apply *dunnage* such as foam, mat, fiber board.

Pallets

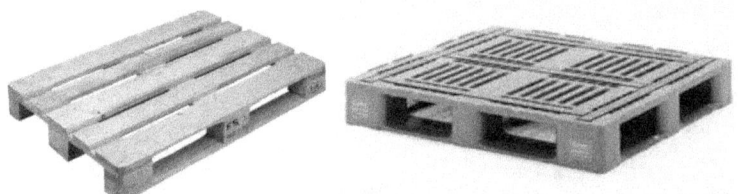

source:http://blog.craftsforum.co.uk/2012/02/09/a-pallet-palace/
source: http://www.logismarket.co.uk

Practical Insight 9.1
Big C moves food without refrigeration

Shipments of fresh products have required refrigerated trucks, involving high rate of fuel consumption and carbon emissions. Big C Supercenter has introduced "Thermal Pallet Cover" to transport fresh food by road hoping to reduce carbon emission from refrigerated trucks by up to 28 per cent.

Source: The Nation April 20, 2011

Roll-on/roll-off (RORO or ro-ro) vessels are designed to carry wheeled cargo such as automobiles, trucks, semi-trailer trucks, trailers or railroad cars. This is in contrast to lo-lo (lift on-lift off) vessels which use a crane to load and unload cargo.

RORO vessels have built-in ramps which allow the cargo to be efficiently "rolled on" and "rolled off" the vessel when import.

RORO

Source: **www.keywordpicture.com** **Source:www.universalcargo.com**

Barge-carrying vessels: The barge-carrying ship is the most recently developed form of cargo unitization. It is also one of the most flexible forms, since it does not need specialized port facilities. For cargo loading each barge is towed out by tugging to the mother ship which hoists the complete unit - barge and goods – on board for the sea journey.

Barge

Source: Author   source: **www.fr.wikipedia.com** © Rémi Jouan

Cargo Handling

Containers are taken off the truck's chassis by cranes at the port of origin and fitted like Lego bricks below and on the deck of the container ship. At the port of disembarking, trucks pull up alongside the ship and containers are lifted by cranes and fitted directly on the chassis. The process is called lift-on, lift-off or LOLO. With RORO, the trailers are rollers

---

that are rolled on board the ship together with the chassis; both units are transported from the origin to the destination.

Typically, a container is cleaned, checked for soundness (no water leakage, good outside physical appearance, etc) packed, locked and sealed, and sent to the destination. It may be moved by road or rail and then by ocean and is usually not opened until it reaches the importing country or sometimes even the importer's warehouse.

Containers are also used for airfreight. Due to large variations in the inside dimensions of aircraft, several standard sizes of containers are used in airfreight.

Container seal

Source: Author

Different Mode of Transportation

When an exporter wishes to send his goods to another country he may have a choice of transportation. Goods can be shipped by surface (road, rail, or sea) or by air. By far the most important method for developing countries is sea, with airfreight as an occasional option.

Road Transportation (Road Haulage)

Road haulage is commonly used in cross-border deliveries and inland delivery of goods to the port of export or from port of import to inland destination. Delivery charge is called cartage or drayage. The trucking company issues a road waybill (also called road consignment note). In some countries, there are legal limitations to the overall height and load of a vehicle on freeways and major roads. Thus transportation of bulk cargo may not be suitable. Specialized forwarders offer consolidation services for local road transport. (Truck load, TL, FTL, LTL, Car load, CL, FCL, LCL)

TIR Carnet (Transport International Routier) is an international transit system for goods carried by road. It was created to allow trucks or lorries carrying international cargos to pass through intervening countries without having to go through customs control procedures. At least one part of the transport operation must be carried out by road, which means that the multimodal transport can be included. The TIR System was designed to speed up border - crossing. It is based on an international treaty, the TIR Convention of 1975, which was drawn up under the auspices of the United Nations.

The system has now 68 contracting parties, mostly in Europe, the Middle East and Central Asia. It is the only transit system with a worldwide vocation. The TIR Convention is operational today in 57 countries. It is based on five principles:

1. Secure vehicles or containers: Goods should travel in secure vehicles or containers.

2. International Chain of Guarantee: Duties and taxes "at risk" during the journey should be covered by an internationally valid guarantee.

3. TIR Carnet: Goods should be accompanied by The TIR carnet taken into use in the country of departure serving as a control document in the countries of departure, transit, and destination.

4. Mutual recognition of customs controls: Customs control measures taken in the country of departure should be accepted by the countries of transit and destination.

5. Controlled access: Access to the TIR system for national issuing and guaranteeing associations is given by the competent national authorities, and for transport

operators, by the national customs authorities and the national association.

The TIR carnet offers the following main benefits:

<u>For international trade:</u> It allows the goods forming the subject of the transaction between private entities to be put into tax-free circulation between two or more countries.

<u>For the transport operation:</u> It offers the transport operator the possibility of putting the load under customs control within the country of departure and enables him to cross the various frontiers with extremely rapid customs controls (saving time).

<u>For the Customs authorities:</u> It offers the guarantee that, if the goods "disappear" on their territory, they can recover from the chain of guarantee the total amount of the Customs duties up to a maximum of US $ 50,000 per TIR Carnet.

Types of Vehicles

Different kinds of vehicles are used in road transportation. They are

<u>Line-Haul vehicles</u>: are tractor trailers combinations of three or more axles. The cargo carrying capacity of these vehicles depends on the size (length) and the state maximum weight limit.

Source: Author

<u>City Straight trucks</u>: are normally smaller than line-haul vehicles. They have cargo and power unit combined in one vehicle. They are usually used in LCL shipments.

Source: Author

Rail Transportation

Rail transportation is popular in multimodal transport and trans-shipment. They are widely used in landbridges. They are popular in transport of bulk cargo in long distance land travel since rail wagons can carry tremendous weight. They are a preferred choice for bulk transport of industrial ore and liquids.

Rail cars, rail wagons (40' to 89' long and can run at 120 km) are available. Piggybacks (trailer on flatcar, TOFC and container on flatcar, COFC) are designed to carry road trailers. Rail waybill or rail consignment bill are used in rail transportation.

Rail transport is less flexible in terms of the total number of shippers, and consignees that can be directly reached, loading is generally not easy and different countries use different rail widths, tunnel clearances, thus requires transshipment

Rail cars

Source:steoil.com   source:railbridge.com

Ocean Transportation

Ocean freight is the most widely used form of transportation in international trade. It still has the attraction of being a cheap mode of transport for delivering large quantities of goods over long distances.

Types of Vessels

Full container ships: are ships that carry all of their load in truck-size intermodal container. Container ships are distinguished into seven major size categories: small feeder, feeder, feedermax, panama, post-panamax, new panamax and ultra-large. Some examples of containership operators are:

- Maersk Line – Denmark
- MSC – Switzerland
- CMA CGM Group – France
- Evergreen Line – Taiwan
- APL – Singapore
- COSCO – China
- Hapag-Lloyd Group – Germany
- CSCL – China
- Hanjin -Rep. of Korea
- NYK – Japan

Container ships

Source: marineinsight.com   source: flickr.com   source: jiyolive.com

Ro-RoRoll-on/roll-off (RORO or ro-ro): are ferries designed to carry wheeled cargo such as automobiles, trucks, trailers or railroad cars. There are different kinds of roro such as ROPAX, ConRO, Pure car carrier and Pure truck carrier.

LASH (Lighter, unpowered barge, Aboard SHip): Lighters can float and be towed up and down a river or canal. Carrier ships are known as LASH which is used where there are inland bridges, thus larger ocean-going vessels cannot be used.

LASH is a liner that carries barges that are loaded at an inland river and shallow ports. Then, the barges are towed to the ocean port's fleeting areas to meet the LASH mother vessel. On arrival, the lighters are individually lifted onto the carrier ship by a large crane located at the stern of the ship. The crane can move the entire length of the ship and stack the lighters atop each other in the ship's body and on the deck. LASH cargo does not require transshipment, as the movement from the origin to destination takes place with a single bill of loading. The system also relieves the pressure to unload as quickly as possible, since the lighters already in the water can be moved while others are being unloaded.

LASH

Source: Author

Bulk carriers are usually employed in tramp service. They are used to carry coal, grain, and other loose cargo.

Bulk carrier and bulk cargo

Source: Author

Tankers are ideally suited to carry liquid cargo. Tankers are fitted with in-laid pipelines with cleaning and cooling equipment.

Tanker

Source: polyar.no   source: **www.foxoildrilling.com**

There are two types of ocean service.

Conference line vessels (LINERS). Groups of shipping companies serve specific ocean routes and ports to standardize prices and practices in ocean transportation worldwide. Liners services are either containers or break-bulk types. They offer the following advantages to shippers:
- common freight rate (tariff) for all shippers
- regular sailing schedule for all ports of call
- stable freight rates for a long period of time, which helps the shippers to quote C&F prices with confidence
- coverage of wide range of ports
- freight rates are normally not negotiable but rebates or discounts to FF are offered.

The following diagram shows the example of ocean shipping route.

Asean Gulf ISC Servic (AGI) of OOCL line

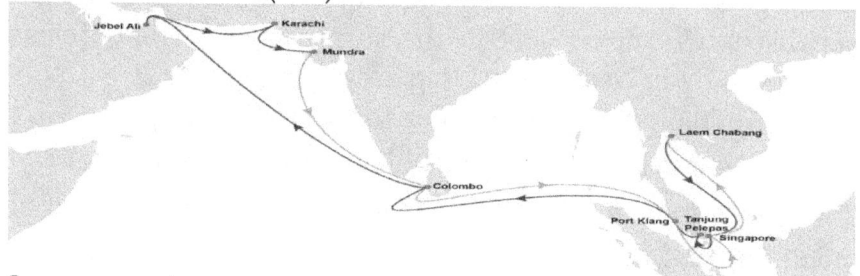

Source: www.oocl.com

Non-conferences vessels (Charter ships and Tramp ships):

These are ships operated by shipping companies. These ships do not follow regular routes but travel as and where cargoes are available. Tramp ships have the following characteristics:

- Voyage routes and schedules are flexible; ships will call at any port.
- They carry whatever cargoes are available.
- They can be hired to transport products for a particular purpose or time.
- They are usually justified for a large order.
- Tramps usually carry homogeneous cargoes like grains, ores, coal, timer, fertilizers, etc.
- Tramps are usually hired for one-way movement of cargo. They do not often get any suitable cargo for their return voyage. In such cases, they compete liners by undercutting the rates and try to get cargo for their return voyage.

The charter party contract is only a contract of carriage, and is thus distinct from a bill of lading. Thus a bill of lading issued under a charter party is not acceptable by banks under letters of credit unless so authorized in the credit. In gross form of charter, the ship owner pays for loading and discharging. Under net terms of charter, the cargo is loaded and discharged at no cost to the ship owner. Trade Terms used specially in charter shipping are

- *FI: Free In* (shipper is responsible for cost of loading)
- *FO: Free out* (shipper is responsible for cost of unloading)
- *FIO: Free In and Out* (shipper is responsible for cost of loading and unloading)

Types of Cargo

In ocean freight, the main types of merchandise (cargo) can be classified into 3 types: - general cargo are merchandise that can be packed in bags, cases, crates, bailings/bundles, pieces & drums and also can be stuffed in a container. General cargos are usually transported by using liner service. Bulk Cargo consists of iron ore & ore concentrates, grain such as rice, corn and bean, coal, phosphate (Fertilizer (can be in rock form)),and others such as pig-iron. Bulk cargos are usually transported by using charter or tramp services. Special type cargo such as RORO cargos which are wheeled cargos.

How the shipping company charges for the freight

The shipping company will charge either by *weight* **(W)** or *measure* **(M),** whichever is greater. In the case of a particularly valuable cargo, the shipping company may charge **an *ad valorem* freight rate** which is calculated on a percentage of the cargo's value. For example, a 2% ad valorem rate on a consignment valued at USD 1000 would raise USD 20. A *minimum* charge may apply to freight charges if the goods are too small for a shipping company to handle them.

Sea carriers commonly levy certain **surcharges** on the basic freight. The most common surcharges are the Bunker Adjustment Factor (BAF) which allows the carrier to adjust freight according to fuel price fluctuations and Currency Adjustment Factor (CAF), for fluctuations in the exchange rate of the currency in which the freight is quoted. The basic freight is usually fixed for periods up to six months or one year and BAF and CAF are subject to overnight revisions. There are various types of freight such as

Container freight: There are two separate cost elements – the rental of the container and the freight. Frequently, the rental of containers provided by the carrier is included in the freight.

Advance freight: is payable in advance, before delivery of the actual goods. This is generally regarded as the most important type of freight and is extensively used in the liner cargo trades and tramping.

Lump Sum freight: The amount payable for the use of the whole or portion of a ship. This form of freight is calculated on the actual cubic capacity of the ship offered and has no direct relation to the cargo to be carried. Lump sum freight is payable irrespective of the actual quantity delivered.

Dead Freight: is claimed for the unoccupied space. If a shipper may fail to provide all the cargo promised and for which space has been reserved on a particular sailing, in which case the ship owner would again claim dead freight for the unoccupied space.

Back Freight: arises when goods have been dispatched to a certain port, and on arrival are refused. The freight charge for the return of the goods constitutes back freight.

Pro rata Freight: arises when the cargo has been carried only part of the way and circumstances make it impossible to continue the voyage further. The point then arises whether the freight calculated pro rate for the portion of the voyage actually accomplished becomes payable.

Container Transport Status

Full container load, FCL: For the FCL shipments, an empty container is taken out from the Container Yard, CY and sent to the exporter's premises and then goods are loaded (stuffed). After the container has been stuffed, it is closed with the carrier's seal.

Less than the container load, LCL: For LCL shipments, exporters deliver the goods to a container terminal, also called Container Freight Station, CFS, where the LCL cargo is grouped together with other LCL cargo sufficient enough to stuff a container. At the terminal near the destination port, the cargo is unloaded from the container and broken down into separate consignments. CFS are located at the port or even far inland. The following diagram 9.6 and 9.7 shows CFS and CY respectively.

Diagram 9.4 Container Freight Stations (CFS)

Source: Author

Diagram 9.5 Container Yard (CY)

Source: Author

The followings are container statuses which are usually found on the transportation documents.

Abbreviation (Europe)	Abbreviation (US)
a) LCL/LCL	CFS/CFS or PIER TO PIER
b) LCL/FCL	CFS/CY or PIER TO HOUSE
c) FCL/FCL	CY/CY or HOUSE TO HOUSE

d) FCL/LCL   CY/CFS or HOUSE TO PIER

a) LCL/LCL or CFS/CFS: This is a situation whereby the shipper stuffs the goods at the container freight station in the country of origin, since the goods delivered cannot fill in a full container capacity. The consignment (the first "LCL") will have to be combined with other shippers' merchandise (the second "LCL"). When the vessel arrives at the destination, the consignee will collect the shipment at the port of destination.

b) LCL/FCL or CFS/CY: This indicates that the shipper stuffs the merchandise at the CFS and the consignee takes the container and unstuffs the shipment at consignee's warehouse.

c) FCL/FCL or CY/CY: This term informs the concerned parties that the shipper takes the container and loads, stows and counts the merchandise at his/her factory and at the destination, the consignee also takes the container, unloads, stows and counts at the consignee's warehouse.

d) FCL/LCL or CY/CFS: The difference between c) and d) is at the destination, where the consignee unstuffs the container at the port of destination.

Basic commercial practice in sea transport
The procedures for arranging a shipment of goods can be complex. The followings are the basic commercial practices in sea transportation.
1. Shipper concludes a contract with the consignee (importer) (with CIF Incoterms 2000).
2. The shipper contacts a freight forwarder to arrange the transport.

3. The forwarder makes enquiries to determine the dates and places of sailing.
4. The forwarder reserves the space on a particular vessel and appropriately fills in a set of pre-printed B/L. The exporter sends shipping particulars to a liner providing information on the departure date, numbers of packages shipped, dimensions of goods and etc.
5. The freight forwarder registers the details on customs entry forms and sends to customs.
6. The Shipper arranges adequate packing, including shipping marks.
7. The shipper, with the forwarder's assistance, will make sure that the goods are either delivered alongside the ship or into the care of a port terminal, or warehouse.
8. When the goods are delivered, the shipper will customarily receive receipt documents such as a mate's receipt, dock receipt, cargo quay receipt or wharf finger's note.
9. The ship owner records the details of the goods receipt, as well as any important defects or damages, on the mate's receipt which will be used as a basis for issuing B/L (clean B/L or foul B/L).
10. The ship owner compares the details of the goods loaded (recorded by the ship owner's clerk) with the draft B/L that the forwarder or shipper has provided. If the details match and the goods do not exhibit damage or defects, the ship owner will issue the completed and signed clean bills of lading. The information from the B/L is also recorded on a register carried by the ship itself, called the ship's manifest. The Manifest (a document that states all the merchandise shipped on a vessel) is forwarded to the destination so that preparations for the arrival and

issuance of delivery orders can be done at the disembarking port.)

11. Once the goods have been loaded, the shipper will obtain the marine insurance (CIF terms).

12. The shipper draws the draft, encloses bill of lading and related documents requested in the L/C (for documentary L/C payment terms) and then gives to the customer, or to the bank acting as an intermediary.

13. When the goods arrive at the port of destination, the ship's master will deliver the goods to the first party who present the original B/L. Usually, the importer will present the B/L to the ship's agent, who will then issue a delivery order (D/O); the importer then uses the D/O to obtain release of the goods.

It is uncommon that the documents arrive after the goods arrive. In case goods arrive first before the documents, since a delay in receiving the goods may result in penalties or storage charges, the consignee may ask his bank to issue shipping guarantee (dock receipt endorsement form) to the ship owner, which will protect the ship owner in the event that he incurs liability for delivery to the wrong person. The ship owner will then release the goods against the shipping guarantee.

Air Transportation

Airfreight is one of the most frequent forms of transportation for the exporter due to the availability of air transportation into and out of most countries. It has many advantages over other modes of transport. Generally, airfreight is the most practical form of transportation for goods which have a high unit value - that is, a high ratio of price to weight.

The most obvious advantage of airfreight is the speed of delivery. For many items such as fresh flowers and fruits, it is the only logical mode of transport if your customers are far away.

Air transport may also be vital for carrying fashionable goods that have a short selling life or for seasonal goods. An exporter may find that airfreight can save him storage costs because he may have to maintain a smaller inventory of raw materials or finished goods, particularly in the export market.

Of course, certain goods are not suitable to carry by air, including many bulky goods and raw materials, where the high cost outweighs other advantages of air transportation. Hazardous cargoes are subject to strict regulations for airfreight. As a general rule, the longer the journey for an export shipment, the less favorable the air cargo rate becomes, compared with ocean freight. Four types of air carriers are available for international shippers: air parcel post, express or expedited service, passenger and cargo.

Air parcel post: is provided by the postal service of a country and is designed to handle small packages. The postal service contacts the air carrier to pick up and deliver the items from one country to another. There are restrictions as to the size and weight of the shipment handled by the air parcel post, and these restrictions vary by country.

Express or expedited service (courier service): is provided by the air carriers and is generally restricted to small shipment weighing less than 70 pounds. Examples of courier services are Federal Express, United Parcel Service, TNT and DHL.

Passenger carriers: focus on the movement of passengers but the excess capacity in non-passenger compartment permits the transportation of cargo along with the passenger.

All cargo carriers: specialize in the movement of freight, not passengers. The airplanes are outfitted with larger hatch openings, and cargo compartments. Many air cargo planes have mechanized materials-handling devices on board to permit the movement of heavier cargo inside the plane. Federal Express, UPS are examples of air cargo carriers.

Though the air freight procedure is simpler than the ocean freight, the procedures may take up too much of an exporter's time. Thus he may wish to use the services of **an air cargo agent.**

International Air Transport Association (IATA): It is the world organization of scheduled airlines. The headquarters are in Montreal and in Geneva. Approximately 80% of all airlines are members of IATA. Charter airlines are not eligible for membership.

IATA standardizes the rules and regulations for air carriers throughout the world. Its members carry the bulk of the world's scheduled international and domestic air traffic under the flags of 88 nations and more. IATA's major purpose is to ensure that all airline traffic anywhere moves with the greatest possible speed, safety, convenience and efficiency and with the utmost economy.

Air Cargo
Air cargo can be divided into 3 main types:
1. General Cargo: needs no special care or attention in handling.
2. Special cargo can be damaged during transportation from the country of origin to the country of destination by time, temperature, altitude, toxicity and delicacy of the products. Types of these cargos are: Heavy Cargo (HEA), Live Animals (AVI), Perishables (PER), Diplomatic Mail (DIP), Valuable cargo (VAL), Human Remains (HUM) and Dangerous Goods (DG).
3. Service Cargo: Merchandise shipped by air that belongs to the airline and/or its staff members.

Air Freight Rates

Airfreight rates vary more than shipping rates but the basis of calculation is usually a price per kilogram (or 427 cubic inches) with certain minimum charges. IATA rates are the published rates that are officially given as guidelines in general airfreight calculation. Under IATA schedules, freight rates decreases according to the weight bracket of the shipment.

Minimum Charge (M Rate): When the weight or volume of a consignment is lower than the minimum weight (0.5kg) or volume, the minimum charge shall apply. Normal Rate (N Rate): is applied when the cargo weight is in between 0.05-45kg. Quantity Rate (Q Rate) is applied for general cargoes which have the weight break equal to or >45kg. Fuel surcharges are additional charges most airlines apply during the increased oil prices.

Unlike ocean freight, it is very seldom that air carriers have direct dealing sales and marketing contacts with shippers or exporters. Most of the time, a freight forwarder is an important intermediary. The following Table 9.1 shows the air freight calculation.

Table 9.1 Air Cargo rates

Air Cargo Rates from Bangkok						
General Cargo Rate (per kg)						
Minimum Charge (0-0.5kg)			N Rate (0.5-45kg)		Q Rate (more than 45kg)	
	US$	Baht	US$	Baht	US$	Baht
Amsterdam	40	1,400	7	253	5.5	190
Hong Kong	20	700	1.5	53	1	35
London	40	1,400	8	276	6	207
Singapore	20	700	1	35	1	35
Tokyo	23	800	3.5	123	2.5	92

Source: Thai Airways International, December 2006, www.thaiairways.com

Pipe Line Transportation

Industries in the Pipeline Transportation subsector use transmission pipelines to transport products, such as crude oil, natural gas, refined petroleum products, and slurry. Pipelines offer high service level (high consistency time delivery, low loss and damage) with low cost. Climate condition has minimal effects on products moving in pipeline. Pipelines are not labor-intensive; therefore, strikes or employee absences have little effect on their operations. Hence, transportation networks include several compressor stations in gas lines or pump stations for crude and multi products pipelines.

Choosing the Right Transportation Mode

In the great majority of cases, geography, availability of services and the physical characteristics of the product will leave the exporter little choice as to which mode of transport he chooses. The major choice is likely to lie between sea and air transport. Road and rail may be used for exports to countries on the same continent. However, for most exporters in developing countries, road and rail transport are primarily a means of moving goods to and from docks or airports.

References
– Cioarec, V. (2007). What transport documents meet the requirements of Art.19 of UCP 600? http://www.forwarderlaw.com/library/view.php?article_id=4 56, accessed on 19 November 2010.
– Thongrung, W. (2010, 2 November 2010). Ministry plans more intermodal dry ports. *The Nation*.
– UNESCAP, T. M. (2011). Multimodal transport operation. Retrieved from http://www.unescap.org/ttdw/CapBuild/ Module%20Multimodal% 20Transport% 20Operations.pdf

10 Export Import Insurance

All experienced exporters are aware of the risks to their cargos while they are in transit. These include fire, storm, collision, pilferage, leakage and explosions. Goods travelling to another country must be insured against loss or damage at each stage of their journey, so that whatever mode of transport is being used, neither the exporter nor the importer suffers any loss. Thus export import insurance plays critical role in international trade. There are two types of export import insurance: export import cargo insurance and export credit insurance.

Export- Import Cargo Insurance

The term cargo insurance, popularly known as marine insurance, applies to all modes of transportation. Proof of insurance coverage is contained in a document known as policy or insurance policy. An insurance policy is issued when goods are insured. The policy must be issued and signed by an insurance company or its agent, the insurer. A policy is a contract, a legal document, and principally it serves as evidence of the agreement between the insurer and the person taking out insurance. The marine insurance policy or certificate forms part of the shipping documents. If more than one original is issued and is so indicated in the policy, all the originals must be presented to the bank, unless otherwise authorized in the L/C.

Under the CIF Incoterms 2010, the exporter must respect an Incoterms requirement to obtain insurance coverage for 110% of the value of the goods. The extra 10% is meant to cover the minimum profit anticipated by the importer. It is also possible to request greater coverage.

The need for export (or import) cargo insurance often differs from exporter to exporter (or importer to importer) and from consignment to consignment.

The liability laid down in the terms of delivery normally conforms to when the title of ownership to the goods passes from the exporter to the customer. This is known as the passing of risk. Insurance can be arranged by an insurance broker or an insurance company. In some countries, import and/or export shipments are insured with their national insurance companies.

There are two kinds of cargo insurance policy.

1. **Open policy, blanket policy, floating policy:** is issued once by the insurer under contract to cover all shipments made by the exporter over a period of time which is subject to renewal, rather than to one shipment only. It is more often used by a large exporter, **assured**. The exporter is required to periodically (usually monthly) declare every shipment made to any location, covering any types of goods, and using any means of conveyance, in order that the insurer may calculate premiums and invoice them accordingly.

2. **Specific policy, voyage policy:** is issued by the insurer to cover a particular shipment or one shipment only.

Whether open policy or specific policy is used by assured, these policies work on three principles of cargo insurance. They are

1. Principles of insurable interest: When the goods are lost or damaged and the owner of the goods (i.e., the title holder of the goods) suffers a loss, fails to realize an expected profit, or incurs liability from the loss or damage, the owner (the title holder) is deemed to have an insurable interest in the goods. The seller will have insurable interest in the goods up to the transfer of risk point, and the buyer will have an insurable interest thereafter. When the exporter delivers the goods, the insurable interest in such

goods transfers at the point and time where the risk shifts from the exporter to the importer, as determined by the INCOTERMS used. For example, the point and time where the risk shifts in:

- FOB: insurable interest transfer from exporter to importer at the time the goods pass over the ship's rail
- CIF: insurable interest transfer from exporter to importer at the time the goods have been delivered on board the shipping vessel.
- CIP: at the time goods are loaded on truck or container, rail care or airplane at the name port of departure.
- DDU/DDP: the exporter is responsible for the risk up to the importer's premises as such the insurable interest in goods does not transfer from the exporter to the importer in the shipment.

2. <u>Utmost good faith</u>: is obligatory in any insurance contract. Under the open policy the insurer usually knows only of the shipments made by the exporter after the receipt of the insurance declaration form. Under such circumstances, a consignment may have reached the importer in:

- **good condition**, that is, without sustaining any loss or damage, before the insurer knows of such consignment. If the exporter knows that the consignment has safely reached the importer and deliberately does not declare such consignment in the insurance declaration form in order to avoid paying the insurance premium, such action is a breach of good faith. Consequently, the insurer may cancel the insurance policy issued to the exporter when the exporter's bad faith is known.
- **bad condition**, that is, sustaining loss or damage, before the insurer knows of such consignment. Whether or not the exporter knows that the consignment has not safely reached the importer and fails to declare such consignment in the insurance declaration form, the

insurer is liable to pay for the loss or damage out of good faith.

3. Indemnity (protection against future loss): Cargo insurance is a contract of indemnity, that is, to compensate for the loss or damage in terms of the value of the insured goods. The amount insured as agreed between the insurer and the assured forms the basis of indemnity.

There are three coverage under marine insurance.

1. **Total coverage:** A policy may pay for sea-water damage only if the loss is **total** (fully damaged) or if the vessel has been stranded, sunk, burnt, or in a collision.

2. **Particular average:** A more inclusive policy which pays for **partial** loss suffered by part of the cargo. (Particular means partial coverage, average means loss)

3. **General average** is a loss that affects all cargo interests on the ship, and the ship itself. General average has been defined as 'a partial and deliberate sacrifice of the ship, freight, or goods, undertaken for the common safety of the adventure in time of peril and/or extraordinary expenditure with the like object.

The idea of general average liability is to spread the losses suffered by only some individuals involved in a voyage, so that all interested parties assume their fair share. If, for example, a ship flounders in a storm and some of the cargo are thrown overboard to save it the resulting loss is considered 'in general average'. The value of the lost goods is contributed proportionately by the parties interested in the voyage – all of the cargo owners and the ship owners. Each of them is required to pay a share of the damage, even though his own cargo may not have been lost or damaged at all.

Accidents often result in both general average and particular average losses. Take the example of a fire in a cargo hold. The ship's crew puts out the fire with water. Some of the cargos in the hold are damaged by the fire itself. This is a **particular average loss.** If the owners of the fire-damaged cargo are insured against this kind of peril, they will be paid for the loss by their insurance company. But cargo in the hold has also been damaged by water used to put the fire out. This is a **general average loss.** Whether or not the owners of the damaged cargo are insured for this kind of damage, they will be largely reimbursed for the loss by contributions from all the other cargo owners and from the ship owners.

Types of Cargo Insurance

The extent of possible insurance coverage that may be purchased varies; there is a wide variety of standard types of coverage. The standard cargo insurance has three basic policies which are All risks, With Particular Average and Free of Particular Average. The **Institute Cargo Clauses** specifically excludes the risks of war and the risks of strikes, riots and civil commotions. The risks of delay in delivery and inherent vice are not included in the clauses.

1. **Institute cargo clauses (All risks):** It covers all risks of physical loss or damage from any external causes irrespective of percentage. The term All Risks is misleading as not all the risks are covered.

It covers against losses caused by the perils of the sea (i.e., the vessel has been stranded, sunk, burnt or been in a collision with other vessels or external substances other than water, such as ice), jettison of cargo, barratry (i.e., negligence, fraud or wrongful acts of the ship's master and/or crew resulting in injury or loss to the ship's owner), and other like perils. If the assured wishes to be covered against the risks of war, strikes, riots, and civil commotions, the insurer deletes the exclusions in the Institute Cargo Clauses and endorses the special clauses, that is, the Institute War Clauses and the Institute Strike Clauses, in the insurance policy and the assured pays an additional premium.

2. **Institute cargo clauses** *(with average, with particular average)*. The With Average is a less inclusive form of coverage than the All Risks. It covers against the total loss and partial loss caused by the perils of the sea, jettison of cargo, barratry, and other like perils.

The partial loss, however, is subject to a franchise being written into the policy. The percentage of franchise can be 3% (or other percentage as specified) of the value of the shipment as agreed between the insurer and the assured. If the loss is less than the indicated franchise of 3% (or other percentage as specified) the assured cannot claim the loss. However, if the loss is equal to or more than the indicated franchise, the assured can claim the loss in full amount without any deduction from the insurer.

Instead of a franchise the insurer and the assured may agree on an excess (deductible). The percentage of excess can be 3-10%. If the loss is equal to or less than the indicated excess, the assured bears the loss, that is, cannot claim the loss. However, if the loss is more than the indicated excess, the assured can claim the loss minus the deduction of the percentage of excess specified. In other words, the assured will always shoulder a percentage of the loss regardless of the amount of the loss.

3. **Institute cargo clauses FPA** *(free of particular average)*. This is the minimum coverage in general use. It covers losses due to a ship or aircraft being totally lost. Partial loss is *not* covered, except to a limited extent and in particular circumstances; which partial losses are covered and under what conditions vary according to national practice.

Marine insurance does not cover the kind of damage that can be expected to occur under normal conditions because of the nature of the goods themselves – their 'inherent vice'. For example, if butter turns rancid during a voyage, which is not interrupted by an accident, this damage would be considered a result of its inherent vice, and would not be covered by the policy. Another case of inherent vice would be fragile glassware inadequately packed. Breakage would be due to its inherent vice – in other words, to internal rather than external causes – even if the packages were handled roughly. Inherent vice is specially excluded from coverage in All Risk clauses, and it is an implied exclusion in all insurance policies, whether or not it is specially mentioned.

Delay is another exclusion that is usually specifically stated, and it is implied in all policies in any case. This means that if goods are delayed in transit and there is a loss because the delay causes them to spoil or lose market value, this loss is not covered. In the case of especially sensitive products, such as meat or butter, it is possible to have the policy changed to pay for physical damage caused by delay, but even then the delay usually must be the result of accidental named perils.

Products should be insured in the appropriate category. A good rule of thumb is that an exporter should insure for the coverage accepted in his particular trade. The seller usually obtains insurance on the minimum coverage as additional coverage is the responsibility of the buyer.

There are New Institute Cargo Clauses namely Institute Cargo Clause (A), (B) and (C). The new clauses are not exact replacements of the old clauses. Some companies may still use the old clauses. The counterparts of the new cargo clauses are as follows in Table 10.1:

Table 10.1 New Cargo Clauses vs Old Cargo Clauses

New Cargo Clauses	Old Cargo Clauses
Institute Cargo Clause (A) ← Institute Cargo Clause (All Risks)	
Institute Cargo Clause (B) ← Institute Cargo Clause (With Average)	
Institute Cargo Clause (C) ← Institute Cargo Clause (Free of particular Average)	

Table 10.2 compares Institute Cargo Clauses (A), (B) and (C)

Table 10.2 Comparison of Institute Cargo Clauses (A), (B) and (C)

⚘ Risks covered   ★ Risks not covered (or Exclusion)

Risk covered and the Exclusion	Institute Cargo Clauses		
	(A)	(B)	(C)
Loss or damage to the subject matter insured approximately caused by [in Clauses (A)] and reasonably attributable to [in Clauses (B) and (C)]:			
Fire or explosion	⚘	⚘	⚘
Vessel or craft stranded, sunk, burnt or capsized	⚘	⚘	⚘
Land conveyance overturned or derailed	⚘	⚘	⚘
Collision or contact of vessel, craft or conveyance with any external object except water	⚘	⚘	⚘
Discharge of cargo at port of distress	⚘	⚘	⚘
Earthquake, lightning or volcanic eruption	⚘	⚘	★
Malicious damage	⚘	★	★
Theft	⚘	★	★
Delay	★	★	★
Inherent vice or nature of the subject matter insured	★	★	★
Willful misconduct of the assured	★	★	★

Loss or damage to the subject matter insured caused by:	Institute Cargo Clauses		
	(A)	(B)	(C)
General average sacrifice	☾	☾	☾
Jettison	☾	☾	☾
Washing overboard	☾	☾	✹
Entry of sea, river or lake water into vessel, craft, conveyance, container or place of storage	☾	☾	✹
Total loss of any package lost overboard or dropped whilst loading on to, or unloading from, vessel or craft	☾	☾	✹
Piracy	☾	✹	✹
War	☾	✹	✹
Strikes, riots and civil commotions, includes terrorists or any persons acting from a political motive	✹	✹	✹
Use of any atomic or nuclear weapon	✹	✹	✹
Ordinary leakage, ordinary loss in weight or volume, or ordinary wear and tear	✹	✹	✹
Insufficiency or unsuitability of packing	✹	✹	✹
The assured privy to the un-seaworthiness of vessel or craft and/or unfitness of vessel, craft, conveyance or container at the time of loading	✹	✹	✹
Insolvency or financial default of the owners or operators of the vessel	✹	✹	✹

Source: adopted from www.export911.com

Insurance Application: The following information is needed while applying for insurance.

- " Name of the assured (Beneficiary - Payable to the order of) "
- " Amount insured "
- Unless otherwise stipulated in the letter of credit (L/C), the minimum amount of insurance coverage the insurance document must indicate should be the CIF or the CIP value of the goods, as the case may be, plus 10%.

- If the CIF or the CIP value cannot be determined, the minimum amount of insurance coverage would be 110% of the amount requested under the L/C for payment, acceptance or negotiation, or 110% of the total amount of the invoice, whichever is the greater. The insurance coverage of 10% more than the CIF or the CIP value is intended as insurance against the loss of expected profit. The L/C may call for an amount of insurance coverage over 110% as settled between the exporter and importer, for example, 120% CIF value or 130% CIP value.
- " Terms of insurance coverage (Clauses) "
- " Latest issuing date of insurance policy"
- "Claim agent" Indicate complete name and address of claim agent at port of destination" " Indicate claims payable in (city, country) in currency "

The following is the insurance claim procedure
1. Report the loss or damage immediately upon taking delivery of your cargo. Whenever your shipment is insured, you should first contact your insurance company and report the loss or damage to them. Then notify the shipping company.
2. Arrange for a survey of the damaged cargo (preferably while the cargo is still untouched). If possible, this should be a joint survey together with the shipping company.
3. The extent and possible cause of the damage must be considered before submitting a fully documented claim with your insurance company or the shipping company directly if your cargo is not insured.

4. When the shipping company receives the claim, the company will acknowledge receipt and the claim will then be processed.
5. The shipping company will let you know its finding as soon as possible. The claim will be assessed according to its nature and the governing laws.
6. The claimant has the burden of verifying the claim. One must produce evidence to show that the loss or damage was caused by insured perils and prove the extent of the claim.

Export Credit Insurance

The insurance covers commercial risks ranging from a buyer's bankruptcy or refusal to pay or take the delivery of the goods to political risks such as restriction or prohibitions on currency remittance and wars, riots, and revolutions. Small exporters face higher risks of non-payment than larger firms do. However, all exporters exporting to new markets or making deals with new importers are also recommended to buy export credit insurance. Export Import Bank of Thailand has offered export credit insurance (EXIMSure) since 1995.

11 Export Import Marketing

In doing international business, elements of the marketing mix - product, price, place, and promotion – needs to be handled with care. Regional, country or local characteristics, product characteristics, and company consideration define whether and to what extent modification is to be made in the marketing mix.

Standardization vs Adaptation

Some factors encourage standardization such as economies in product R&D, economies of scale in production, economies in marketing, control of marketing programs, convergence of customers' preferences and "shrinking" of the world marketplace. On the other hand, some other factors encourage adaptation such as differing use conditions, government and regulatory influences, differing buyer behavior patterns, local initiative and motivation in implementation and adherence to the marketing concept.

Product Policy

Products offer bundles of attributes. When product attributes and customer's needs match, that product will be successful in the market. If the customer's needs are the same all over the world, standardized products can be sold in all international markets without adaptation. However, countries differ in terms of culture, social behaviors, economy and so on, therefore, some firms have to adapt their products.

Pricing Policy

Basically, firms are using three basic pricing policies such as cost leadership, differentiation, or focus. International pricing policy must match the firm's overall pricing policy. International marketing price setting strategies include

- Standard worldwide pricing - average unit costs of fixed, variable, and export-related costs. Firms set single selling price for all international markets. Local production cost, export, distribution cost, local purchasing power and exchange rate differences make standard worldwide pricing difficult.
- Dual pricing - export price differs from the domestic price. (cost-plus method or marginal cost method). Due to the inability to fully separate international buyers from the domestic buyers, grey markets exist.

There are some issues in international pricing; such as transfer pricing where intra-company product transfers are made. For the custom valuation and classification, the lower the value the exporters set, the lower the tax needed to be paid. In order to avoid such practice, some governments set upper and lower limit for the product price. When the firm sets at low price they might also be accused of dumping. Some firms use arm's length pricing strategy which is free-market price that unrelated parties charge one another for a specific product.

Distribution Policy

In exporting, the exporter can sell the product through many channels.

- Export Merchants: Use their own capital to buy the merchandise from the producers (exporters) for export. They take title of the goods.
- Export Management Company (EMC): Performing export functions on behalf of the producers (exporters). All documents will be done under the name of the producers. EMC earns commission from the producer.
- Export Agent: A business unit or person who is doing the selling of merchandise on behalf of the producers (exporters) to foreign buyers. They neither hold any

inventory nor take possession of the goods. They earn commission.

- Export Broker: A company/person who arranges a meeting or trade negotiation between a seller and a buyer. They earn brokerage fee.

In importing as well, there are also many channels through whom importing can be carried on.

- Import Merchant -- same as export merchant
- Import Agent --- same as Export agent
- Buying Agent: A company / person representing an importer to purchase merchandise or goods from foreign countries. They could be established by the importer or be the importer's representative.
- Distributor: A sole purchaser or purchasers appointed by the producers in foreign countries to distribute the products in the local markets. The distributors will sell the product with a profit margin to the local merchants. The distributors will control the selling price for both wholesale and retail.

Nowadays, firms can select digital intermediaries to help them enter the e-commerce arena.

Promotion Policy

A combination of the various promotional tools will create the product and firm's image among the intended target market. Participating in trade fairs and exhibitions is one of the important promotional activities.

Using Integrated Marketing Communication (IMC), the company carefully integrates and coordinates its many communication channels to deliver a clear, consistent, and compelling message about the organization and its brands.

Digital technology revolutionized the media. Digital technology offer consumers a fast track to get news. At the same time, consumers today have shorter attention spans and prefer less text. Technology has liberated the consumer choice. By using technology consumers' lives have been made much easier and faster. Thus the traditional media such as print and television needs to be adopted. For example, some products appearing in the magazines should be able to be purchased on line and on mobiles. Companies need to deliver the right content in the right context to the right target (Rungfapaisarn, 2010).

Reference

- Rungfapaisarn, K. (2010, 3.12.2010). Traditional media need to change ways: study. *The Nation.*

12 Setting up Export Import Business

The following list summarizes one should do in setting up export import business.

- Choose the product or service (internal analysis)
  - Core competencies and value chain analysis
  - Conduct international business research (SWOT analysis)
- External Environmental Analysis (PEST analysis, Competitors' analysis) on the following factors:
  - The fit between the product that the firm would like to offer and the local consumers' preference
  - Political stability and Political factors
  - Importing country restrictions
    - Tax regulations
    - Licensing and other requirements
    - Tariffs and quotas of importing countries
    - Currency Restrictions, stability of local currency
  - Trading agreements between countries and finding out how these agreements are beneficial for the product that you are handling.
  - Any government promotions related to your export/import business
  - Property right implications
  - Exchange rates, foreign exchange control and currency convertibility
  - What is the location of the market, demography of the market?

- What is the climate, geography of the market?
- What is the market size, targeted customers, pattern of the market, product and (past, present & future) growth?
- Infrastructure?
- Who are your competitors? Globally & Locally. (Their SWOT & Your SWOT)
- Etc.
- Make contacts
  - Sourcing (finding) a manufacturer or provider of the product or service you wish to import or export
- Define the terms of sales (Incoterms used)
- Export – Import payment terms
- Customs requirements and rules and regulations of the countries concerned
- One must understand the export – import procedures and parties involved in the procedure and the documentation needed in the whole process.
- Trade financing: One must need to find out whether he/she has enough financing. Where one can get financing for exporting and importing.
- Choosing types of transportation
  - Types of vessel/ types of carriers
  - Shipping / air lines
  - Packaging, containerization, LCL, FCL
- Cargo Insurance policy choice
- Marketing channels and marketing mix strategies

Finally, the cost structure of the whole trade transaction chain is calculated as follows:Table 12.1 Cost Structure of Trade Transaction Chain

Export		Import	
Cost elements	Cost	Cost elements	Cost
Factory cost of *** tons		Land cost CIF	$ ****
@ $ *** per ton	$ ****	Duty @ **%	$ ****
Expenses:		Other Taxes	$ ****
Brokerage costs	$ ****	Brokerage - Clearance fees	$ ****
Export packing	$ ****	Forwarder Fees	$ ****
Freight to port	$ ****	Banking charges	$ ****
Consular invoice	$ ****	Total landed cost (DDP)	$ ****
Freight forwarder Fee	$ ****	Expenses:	
FOB price	$ ****	Warehouse	$ ****
		Repackaging	$ ****
		Freight out	$ ****
		Advertising	$ ****
		Interest	$ ****
		others	$ ****
Marine insurance	$ ****	Total landed plus expenses	$ ****
Transportation (Ocean)	$ ****	Plus Markup	$ ****
Landed cost (CIF)	$ ****	Suggested selling Price	$ ****

Source: Author; Adopted from Nelson, Carl A. (2000)

Appendix

ICC MODEL INTERNATIONAL SALE CONTRACT
(Manufactured Goods Intended for Resale)

A. Specific Conditions

These Specific Conditions have been prepared in order to permit the parties to agree the particular terms of their sale contract by completing the spaces left open or choosing (as the case may be) between the alternatives provided in this document. Obviously this does not prevent the parties from agreeing other terms or further details in box A-16 or in one or more annexes.

SELLER	CONTACT PERSON	**BUYER**	CONTACT PERSON
Name & Address	Name & address	Name & address	Name & address
---------------	------------------------	------------------	----------------------

A-1 GOODS SOLD

(DESCRIPTION OF THE GOODS)

If there is insufficient space parties may use an annex.

A-2 CONTRACT PRICE (ART. 4)

Currency: [　　　　　　　]

Amount in number: [　　　　　　　]   Amount in letter: [　　　　　　　　　　]

A-3 DELIVERY TERMS

Recommended terms (according to Incoterms 2010):

- o **EXW** Ex Works — named place: [　　]
- o **FCA** Free Carrier — named place: [　　]
- o **CPT** Carriage Paid To — named place of destination: [　　]
- o **CIP** Carriage and Insurance Paid To — named place of destination: [　　]
- o **DAT** Delivered at Terminal — Named place of terminal: [　　]
- o **DAP** Delivered at Place — Name place: [　　]
- o **DDP** Delivered Duty Paid — named place of destination: [　　]

Other terms (according to Incoterms 2010)

- o **FAS** Free Alongside Ship — named port of shipment: [　　]
- o **FOB** Free On Board — named port of shipment: [　　]
- o **CFR** Cost and Freight — Named port of destination: [　　]
- o **CIF** Cost Insurance and Freight

Other delivery terms

o

CARRIER (where applicable)

NAME AND ADDRESS   CONTACT PERSON

_____   _____

_____   _____

A-4 TIME OF DELIVERY

Indicate here the date or period (e.g. week or month) at which or within which the Seller must perform his delivery obligations according to clause A.4 of the respective Incoterm (see Introduction, s 6)

A-5 INSPECTION OF THE GOODS BY BUYER (ART. 3)

o   Before shipment   place of inspection: [   ]

o   Other: [   ]

A-6 RETENTION OF TITLE (ART. 7)
o Yes   0 No

A-7 PAYMENT CONDITIONS (ART. 5)

o **Payment on open account (art. 5.1)**

Time for payment (if
different from art. 5.1) [   ] days from date   Other: [   ]
                                        of invoice.
o Open account backed by demand guarantee or standby letter of credit (art. 5.5)

o **Payment in advance (art. 5.2)**

Date (if different from [   ] o Total price [   ] % of the
art. 5.2):   price

o **Documentary Collection (art. 5.5)**

   oD/P Documents against payment   o D/A Documents against
   acceptance

o **Irrevocable Documentary Credit (art. 5.3)** o Confirmed   o Unconfirmed

Place of issue (if applicable): [   ] Place of confirmation
                                             (if applicable): [   ]

Credit available:
- By payment at sight   *Partial shipments:*

   Transhipment:

- By deferred payment at: [_____] days o Allowed   o Allowed
- By acceptance of drafts at: [____] days   o Not allowed   0 Not allowed
- By negotiation

Date on which the documentary credit must be notified to seller (if different from art. 5.3)

- [_____] days before date of delivery   o other: [_____]

o **Other:** [..]

(e.g. cheque, bank draft, electronic funds transfer to designated bank account of seller)

A-8 DOCUMENTS

Indicate here documents to be provided by Seller. Parties are advised to check the Incoterm they have selected under A-3 of these Specific Conditions. (As concerns transport documents, see also Introduction, &8)

o **Transport documents:** indicate type of transport

document required [_____]

o **Commercial Invoice**   o **Certificate of origin**

o **Packing list**   o **Certificate of inspection**

o **Insurance document**   0 **Other** [___]

A-9 CANCELLATION DATE

TO BE COMPLETED ONLY IF THE PARTIES WISH TO MODIFY ARTICLE 10.3

If the goods are not delivered for any reason whatsoever (including force majeure) by (date) [_____] the Buyer will be entitled to CANCEL THE CONTRACT IMMEDIATELY BY NOTIFICATION TO THE SELLER

A-10 LIABILITY FOR DELAY (art. 10.1, 10.4 AND 11.3)

TO BE COMPLETED ONLY IF THE PARTIES WISH TO MODIFY ART. 10.1, 10.4 OR 11.3

Liquidated damages for delay in delivery shall be:

o [____] % (of price of delayed goods) per week, with a maximum of [____] % (of price of delayed goods) **or:**

o [_____] specify amount)

In case of termination for delay, Seller's liability for damages for delay is limited to [_____] % of the price of the non-delivered goods

A-11 LIMITATION OF LIABILITY FOR LACK OF CONFORMITY (ART. 11.5)

TO BE COMPLETED ONLY IF THE PARTIES WISH TO MODIFY ART. 11.5.

Seller's liability for damages arising from lack of conformity of the goods shall be:
o limited to proven loss (including consequential loss, loss of profit, etc.) not
　　exceeding [_____] % of the contract price; **or:**
o as follows (specify): [_____]

A-12 LIMITATION OF LIABILITY WHERE NON-CONFORMING GOODS ARE RETAINED BY THE BUYER(ART. 11.6)
TO BE COMPLETED ONLY IF THE PARTIES WISH TO MODIFY ART. 11.6

The price abatement for retained non-conforming goods shall not exceed:
o [_____] % of the price of such goods **or:**
o [_____] (specify amount)

A-13 TIME-BAR (Art.11.8)

TO BE COMPLETED ONLY IF THE PARTIES WISH TO MODIFY ART. 11.8.
Any action for non-conformity of the goods (as defined in article 11.8) must be taken by the Buyer not later than [_____] from the date of arrival of the goods at destination.

A-14(a), A-14(b) APPLICABLE LAW (Art.1.2)

TO BE COMPLETED ONLY IF THE PARTIES WISH TO SUBMIT THE SALE CONTRACT TO A NATIONAL LAW INSTEAD OF CISG. The solution hereunder is **not** recommended (see Introduction, s 3)
This sales contract is governed by the domestic law of ----------------------
(country)

To be completed if parties wish to choose a law other than that of the seller for questions not covered by CISG
Any questions not covered by CISG will be governed by the law of (country)

A-15 RESOLUTION OF DISPUTES (Art.14)

The two solutions hereunder (arbitration or litigation before ordinary courts) are alternatives: parties cannot choose both of them. If no choice is made, ICC arbitration will apply, according to art. 14

o **ARBITRATION**   O **LITIGATION (ordinary courts)**

   o ICC (according to art. 14.1)   In case of dispute the courts of

        Place of arbitration [＿＿＿＿＿＿]   [＿＿＿＿＿＿＿＿＿] (place)

o Other [＿＿＿＿＿＿＿＿＿] (specify) shall have jurisdiction

A-16 OTHER

The present contract of sale will be governed by these Specific Conditions (to the extent that the relevant boxes have been completed) and by the ICC General Conditions of Sale (Manufactured Goods Intended for Resale) which constitute part B of this document.

SELLER   **BUYER**
(signature)   (signature)

_____   _____

Place _____ Date _____   place _____ date _____

source: Author, adopted from The ICC Model International Sales Contract, 1997 edition, ICC publication N 556

ธนาคารกสิกรไทย
KASIKORNBANK PUBLIC COMPANY LIMITED

APPLICATION FOR ISSUING AN IRREVOCABLE DOCUMENTARY CREDIT

TO : KASIKORNBANK PUBLIC COMPANY LIMITED   DATE: _____
WE HEREBY REQUEST YOU TO ISSUE AN IRREVOCABLE DOCUMENTARY CREDIT ON OUR BEHALF WITH THE FOLLOWING CONDITIONS:

APPLICANT'S NAME AND FULL ADDRESS(:50:)	**BANK USE ONLY**
	INTERNATIONAL TRADE SERVICE OFFICE :
	LC NO(:20:)
	ADVISING BANK:
	THE CREDIT IS (:41D) ( ) RESTRICTED ( ) UNRESTRICTED
TEL: FAX:	THIS CREDIT IS TRANSFERABLE(:40A:) ( ) YES ( ) NO
BENEFICIARY'S NAME AND FULL ADDRESS(:59:)	CONFIRMATION (:49:) ( ) CONFIRM ( ) WITHOUT ( ) MAY ADD
	CONFIRMATION COMMISSION IS FOR A/C OF ( ) APPLICANT ( ) BENEFICIARY
	AVAILABLE BY BENEFICIARY'S DRAFT AT ( ) SIGHT
	( ) TERMS_____
	EXPIRY DATE AND PLACE(:31D:)
TEL: FAX:	SHIPMENT FROM: _____
AMOUNT AND CURRENCY(:32B:) FIGURES AND WORDS: (+/-)_____%	TO:_____
	LATEST SHIPMENT DATE(:44C:)
	TRANSSHIPMENT(:43T:) ( ) ALLOWED ( ) NOT ALLOWED
	PARTIAL SHIPMENTS(:43P:) ( ) ALLOWED ( ) NOT ALLOWED

DOCUMENTS REQUIRED(:45A:)
( )SIGNED COMMERCIAL INVOICE IN _____COPIES, PRICE: ( ) EXW ( )FOB ( )CFR ( )CF
    OR IN CASE SHIP BY AIR/OTHERS   ( )FCA ( )CPT ( )CIP ( )OTHERS_____
PORT/ PLACE: _____INDICATING FOB OR FCA VALUE, FREIGHT AND INSURANCE PREMIUM (IF ANY)
( )FULL SET OF CLEAN ON BOARD BILL OF LADING ( ) MULTIMODAL TRANSPORT DOCUMENT
MADE OUT OR ENDORSED TO THE ORDER OF KASIKORNBANK PCL, MARKED FREIGHT; ( )PREPAID ( )COLLECT NOTIFY APPLICANT,
PLUS _____NON-NEGOTIABLE COPIES
( )AIR WAYBILL ( )POST RECEIPT ( )TRUCK RECEIPT ( )RAILWAY RECEIPT
CONSIGNED TO KASIKORNBANK PCL, MARKED FREIGHT; ( ) PREPAID ( ) COLLECT NOTIFY APPLICANT AND INDICATING L/C NUMBER
( )INSURANCE POLICY OR CERTIFICATE IN DUPLICATE ENDORSED IN BLANK FOR OF INVOICE VALUE, STATING CLAIMS PAYABLE IN
THAILAND FOR CURRENCY OF THE DRAFT(S), COVERING: ( )INSTITUTE CARGO CLAUSES ( )A ( )B ( )C ( )AIR
         ( )INSTITUTE STRIKE CLAUSES (CARGO) ( )INSTITUTE WAR CLAUSES (CARGO)
         ( )THEFT PILFERAGE AND/OR NON-DELIVERY CLAUSES ( )OTHER
( )PACKING LIST IN_____COPIES   ( ) CERTIFICATE OF ORIGIN IN_____COPIES
OTHER DOCUMENTS:_____

DESCRIPTION OF GOODS(:45A:)_____

CHARGES(:71B:) ALL BANK CHARGES INCLUDING REIMBURSING CHARGES AND OTHER EXPENSES INCURRED OUTSIDE THAILAND ARE FOR THE ACCOUNT OF:
( ) APPLICANT   ( ) BENEFICIARY
PRESENTATION PERIOD(:48:) DOCUMENTS MUST BE PRESENTED WITHIN DAYS AFTER SHIPMENT DATE BUT WITHIN VALIDITY OF THE CREDIT.
ADDITIONAL CONDITIONS (:47A:)_____

IN ADDITION TO THE INSTRUCTIONS MENTIONED ABOVE, WE, IN CASE THE TERMS OF PAYMENT UNDER LETTER OF CREDIT IS TO BE PAYABLE AT A FUTURE DATE, AGREE AND AUTHORIZE YOU TO CONFIRM THE DUE DATE TO THE NOMINATED BANK OR ALL PARTIES CONCERNED WITHOUT ANY CONSENT FROM US.
IN CONSIDERATION OF YOUR ISSUING OF THE ABOVE MENTIONED LETTER OF CREDIT, WE HEREBY GUARANTEE TO PAY ALL SUCH DRAFT (S) ON PRESENTATION FOR SIGHT DRAFT (S) AND TO PAY SAME AT MATURITY FOR TIME DRAFT (S)
TOGETHER WITH OTHER CHARGES AND INTEREST AT THE RATE APPLICABLE DEFAULT INTEREST RATE AS ANNOUNCED BY KASIKORNBANK PCL, PROVIDED THAT SUCH RATE SHALL BE SUBJECT TO CHANGE BY KASIKORNBANK PCL, FROM TIME TO TIME.
THE TRANSMISSION OF INSTRUCTIONS UNDER AND/OR IN RELATION TO THIS LETTER OF CREDIT IS ENTIRELY AT OUR OWN RISK. THIS APPLICATION IS SUBJECT TO ADDITIONAL CLAUSES OVERLEAF.
UNLESS OTHERWISE EXPRESSLY STATED, THIS LETTER OF CREDIT IS SUBJECT TO "UNIFORM CUSTOMS AND PRACTICE FOR DOCUMENTARY CREDITS" (2007 REVISION) INTERNATIONAL CHAMBER OF COMMERCE (PUBLICATION NO.600)
WE FURTHER AUTHORIZE YOU TO DEBIT OUR ACCOUNT NO. _____ MAINTAIN WITH YOUR _____
BRANCH FOR THE ISSUING COMMISSION AND OTHER EXPENSES INCURRED WHETHER THE LETTER OF CREDIT HAVE BEEN UTILIZED OR NOT, AND THE AMOUNT OF DRAFT (S) PRESENTED UNDER THIS LETTER OF CREDIT PLUS INTEREST AND CHARGES UNDER ADVICE TO US.

BANK USE ONLY
SIGNATURE VERIFIED BY

PP.RLC 22-04-10

_____
AUTHORIZED SIGNATURE(S) WITH COMPANY SEAL

APPLICATION FOR L/C CONFIRMATION

TO : KASIKORNBANK PUBLIC COMPANY LIMITED : HEAD OFFICE

ATTN : Issue & Advice L/C Unit

DATE :

RE L/C NO.

ISSUED BY :

AMOUNT OF :

YOUR REF.

       WE HEREBY REQUEST YOU TO ADD CONFIRMATION UNDER THE ABOVE MENTIONED L/C ACCORDING TO THE OPENNING BANK INSTRUCTIONS.

ACCORDING TO THE L/C TERMS, ALL EXPENSES CONCERNING THIS MATTER ARE FOR OUR ACCOUNT/APPLICANT'S ACCOUNT. (IN CASE CHARGES ARE FOR APPLICANT, THE BENEFICIARY HAS TO PAY IN ADVANCE AND SHALL BE REFUNDED UPON RECEIPT FROM THE APPLICANT)

       PAYABLE BY CASH
       PLEASE DEBIT OUR ACCOUNT WITH KASIKORNBANK PUBLIC COMPANY LIMITED.
               BRANCH., ACCOUNT NO.

               YOURS FAITHFULLY

               AUTHORIZED SIGNATURE WITH COMPANY'S SEAL

BANK'S SIGNATURE VERIFICATION
THE ABOVE SIGNATURE WITH TITLE AS STATED CONFORMS TO THAT ON FILE
WITH US AND IS AUTHORIZED FOR THE EXECUTION OF SUCH INSTRUMENTS.

NAME OF BANK AND AUTHORIZED SIGNATURE

IN05002-5-01

Source:http://www.kasikornbank.com/TH/ApplyForServices/ApplyForServiceForm/APP
LICATION_FOR_LC_CONFIRMATION_v420081027.pdf

ธนาคารกสิกรไทย
KASIKORNBANK ธนาคาร

APPLICATION FOR TRANSFER OF DOCUMENTARY CREDIT

To **KASIKORNBANK PUBLIC COMPANY LIMITED,**   Date
1 SOI KASIKORNTHAI, RATBURANA ROAD, BANGKOK.
Attention: Issue & Advice L/C Unit

Dear Sirs,

L/C No.	
Your Ref. No.	

We, the undersigned beneficiary of the above L/C, hereby irrevocably you to transfer the said Letter of Credit to the following name and address:

Transferee's Name	
Address	

Under the following terms and conditions:

1	Transferred amount	
2	Covering shipment of	
3	Shipment date must be altered to	
4	The Expiry date must be altered to	
5	Documents must be presented within	days after issuance of the transport document but within the validity of the credit

Special Condition

Applicant's Name   be shown

All bank charges are for account for account of

Negotiation must be restricted to KASIKORNBANK PUBLIC COMPANY LIMITED .,Int'l Trade Center

Please advise the transferred L/C through

We agree to transfer all rights or part thereof as the case may be to the second beneficiary to draw under the above letter of credit and advise all incoming relative amendments to   In case no instruction is given by us, you may advise the relative amendments on your discretions.

Collect your transfer commission and expenses from   by   No. [| | | | -]
                                                                         Branch Name

This transfer is subjected to the Uniform Customs and Practice for Documentary Credit, 1993 Revision, ICC Publication No.500

Yours faithfully,

Authorized Signature with Company's Seal

FOR KBANK USE ONLY	FOR BANK WHO VERIFY THE SIGNATURE
	The above signature with title and company seal as stated conform to that on file with us and is authorized for the execution of such instruments.
	Authorized Signature Code
Checked Approved	Name of Bank

9904026-12-01

COLLECTION/INSTRUCTION FOR NEGOTIATION/DISCOUNT OF EXPORT BILLS

To : **KASIKORNBANK PUBLIC COMPANY LIMITED**   Date

HEAD OFFICE 1 SOI KASIKORNTHAI, RATBURANA ROAD, BANGKOK 10140, THAILAND.
TEL. +66 2222 0000 FAX +66 2470 1144-5

Dear Sirs,

   We hereby request you to dispose of the enclosed draft and documents described below:

   For purchase/negotiation subject to final payment   For payment to us after collection

COLLECTING BANK	Full name & address :		
DRAWER/PRINCIPAL /SELLER	Full name :		
	Postal address :		
	Telex :	Telephone :	Facsimile :
DRAWEE/BUYER	Full name :		
	Postal address :		
	Telex :	Telephone :	Facsimile :
Invoice/Draft no.	Currency & Amount	Tenor	Merchandise
			Despatched VIA s.s voy no

LIST OF DOCUMENTS ENCLOSED

Draft	Invoice	Bill of Lading	Certificate of Origin	Packing List	Insurance Policy	Air Waybill	Weight List	Parcel post Receipt	Inspection Certificate	OTHER DOCUMENTS DENOTED BELOW				
										A	B	C	D	E

A   B   C

D   E

Deliver Documents Against Payment (D/P)	Do not waive charges/interest by drawee
Deliver Document Against Acceptance (D/A)	Payment may be deferred until arrival of goods
Advise Non Payment by Telex/Airmail/Telecommunication	Collect interest as stated on the draft
Advise Non Acceptance by Telex/Airmail/Telecommunication	Case of need : name
Advise Acceptance & Maturity date by Telex/Airmail/	Who is authorized only obtain honouring of drafts as drawn
Telecommunication	Who is authorized to give instructions which are to be
Protest for Non-Payment/Non-Acceptance at our expense	followed in every respect.
All charges for account of Drawee	Advise Non-Compliance of other instructions detailed
Collect interest at % P.A. (360/365 Days)	below by Telex/Airmail/Telecommunication
after first presentation/maturity till payment	Other instructions :

   In consideration of your having discounted/ negotiated or purchased our documentary bill/draft, we hereby undertaken to hold you free and harmless from all losses or damages howsoever caused to you in consequence of non-acceptance and/or non-payment and/or late payment of every bill/draft discounted or purchase or negotiated and we further undertaken to refund to you the foreign currency amount of the bill/draft immediately upon your receipt of notice of non/acceptance and/or non-payment and we hereby authorize you to charge our account with the baht equivalent of the bill/draft at the prevailing Bank's selling rate for the foreign currency amount of the bill/draft together with interest at your maximum default rate for the time being chargeable by you to your customer commencing from the maturity date of the relevant bill/draft up until all indebtedness thereunder shall have been paid in full plus all other costs or expenses thereof.

   When making payment for us please credit our Account No   with your Head Office/Branch

            after deducting our liability under Packing Credit Loan No

with Forward Contract No

   This collection subject to Uniform Rules For Collection (1995 Revision) International Chamber of Commerce (Publication No.522)

Please refer all questions concerning this collection to: Yours faithfully,

Tel No   Fax

                                                                      Authorized Signature

*The maximum default interest rate is defined to mean the maximum interest rate permitted by The Bank of Thailand for commercial bank to charge to its customers according to the Announcement of The Bank of Thailand regarding instruction for commercial banks to perform with respect to interest and discount rate.
   (This is a standard form approved by Thai Banker's Association)

9905161-12-06

**APPLICATION FOR NEGOTIATION / DISCOUNT OF EXPORT BILLS
DRAWN UNDER LETTER OF CREDIT**

To : **KASIKORNBANK PUBLIC COMPANY LIMITED**   Date
HEAD OFFICE 1 SOI KASIKORNTHAI, RATBURANA ROAD, BANGKOK 10140, THAILAND.
TEL. +66 2222 0000 FAX. +66 2470 1144-5

Dear Sirs,

    Re: Our Draft / Invoice No.   date
    for   drawn under L/C No.
    Issued by

We,   , (Insert the company's name)
submit herewith documents for negotiation / discount under the above mentioned Letter of Credit as follows:

DOCUMENTS	B/E	INV.	P/L	C/INV	C/O	INSP CERT	Qual CERT	INS	B/L	AWB	ORIG L/C		

DISPOSITION OF PAYMENT :

    Credit our account No.   after deducting your charges.
    Apply proceeds to our export loan P / C No.   the remaining balance
    (if any) please credit our account No.
    Other instructions:

In consideration of your having negotiated / discounted our above mentioned documents, we hereby agree
as follows:

1. In the event of any delay in payment and / or acceptance of said draft(s) and / or documents, we undertake
    to pay you at the maximum default rate" of interest on the amount of such draft(s) and / or documents.

2. We hereby agree that your negotiation / discount of said draft (s) and / or documents is done on a
    "with recourse" basis. Therefore, in the event of non-payment and / or non-acceptance of said draft(s)
    and / or documents, either by reason of any discrepancy raised by the issuing bank or by other reason
    whatsoever, we undertake to refund to you the foreign currency amount of such draft(s) and / or documents
    together with interest thereon at the maximum default interest rate" from the date of disposition of proceeds
    as above mentioned until full payment thereof.

3. We further undertake to hold you free and harmless from and against all expenses, losses and damages
    howsoever incurred and / or may be incurred to you in consequence of your negotiation / discount of the
    above mentioned documents and to fully indemnify you immediately upon our receipt of your notice to
    that effect.

4. We hereby agree that this will serve as your authority to charge our account with the Baht equivalent of
    the draft(s) and / or documents amount at the then prevailing bank's selling rate including interest and all
    other cost and expenses.

5. We further agree that your negotiation / discount of our above mentioned documents is subject to the Uniform
    Customs and Practice for Documentary Credits (1993 Revision), International Chamber of Commerce,
    (Publication No.500).

Encl :

Yours faithfully,

Forward contract No.

Authorized Signature

"The maximum default interest rate is defined to mean the maximum interest rate permitted by the Bank of Thailand
for commercial bank to charge to its customers according to the Announcement of the Bank of Thailand
regarding instruction for commercial banks to perform with respect to interest and discount rate.

(This is a standard form approved by Thai Banker's Association.)

9904018-10-08

Source:http://www.kasikornbank.com/EN/ApplyForServices/ApplyForServiceForm/APP
LICATION_FOR_NEGOTIATION_DISCOUNT_OF_EXPORT_BILLS.pdf

TRUST RECEIPT

(Hypothecated Shipping Documents)

To : **KASIKORNBANK** PUBLIC COMPANY LIMITED

HEAD OFFICE 1 SOI KASIKORNTHAI, RATBURANA ROAD, BANGKOK 10140, THAILAND.

TEL. +66 2222 0000 FAX. +66 2470 1144-5

Date.....................

In consideration of your handing to me / us Shipping Documents representing the goods specified therein as per particulars at foot, hypothecated to you as collateral security for the due payment of the undermentioned bill (s) / draft (s) payable to you drawn upon me / us by

and accepted by me / us. I / We hereby engage to utilize the same promptly without expense to you for no other purpose other than landing clearing from customs, storing and holding the said goods as Trustee for you and on your behalf and keep the said goods separate and capable of identification from other goods in my / our possession advising you of its location, and in the event of the goods or any portion thereof being sold and delivered before full payment of the said bill (s) / draft (s), the proceeds of such sale shall be received by me / us as Trustee for you, and paid to you when and as received notwithstanding prior to its due date. I / We at the same time will advise you the account on which such payment is made. I / We shall obtain your approval prior to sell the said goods on credit or against any Bill of Exchange or Promissory Note and shall deliver to you such undertaking to pay by buyer thereof or deliver to you such Bill of Exchange or Promissory Note properly endorsed.

I / We also undertake to keep the goods fully insured at my / our expense specifying your name as beneficiary against loss by fire, thefts and any other risk to which said goods may be subject to and to deliver any and all policies to you upon demand.

I / We allow you and anyone authorized by you in writing to enter my / our warehouses and premises or any place where the said goods may be stored at any time for viewing, inspecting, identifying and / or taking possession of the goods for any other purpose relating to this TRUST RECEIPT.

You may at any time cancel this TRUST RECEIPT and take possession of the said goods and in doing so will in no way impair or lessen your rights to receive payment of the full amount of the bill (s) / draft (s) and / or release my / our liability to pay same.

It is agreed that you assume no responsibility for the correctness, validity or genuineness of the documents released to me / us hereunder or for the existence character quantity, quality, conditions, value or delivery of any goods purported to be represented by any of such documents.

It is also agreed that the undermentioned bill (s) / draft (s) will be paid by me / us in full at maturity irrespective of the sale of the said goods.

I / We agree to pay you interest on the outstanding amount of bill (s) / draft (s) at the rate of .... % (........................ percent) per annum. The Payment of interest shall be made on the 26th day of each calendar month ("Interest Payment Date") commencing from the date of this Trust Receipt. If the Interest Payment Date of any calendar month falls on a day which is not a banking day, the Interest Payment Date shall be shortened to the preceding banking day. The last payment of interest shall be due on the maturity date of such bill (s) / draft (s).

If I/We default in any due performance under this Trust Receipt or fail to pay any amount when due, I/We shall pay you default interest on the outstanding amount in Thai Baht currency of bill (s) / draft (s) at the default rate announced by you from time to time which is presently .... % (........................ Percent) per annum. If the outstanding amount of bill (s) / draft (s) is in currency other than Thai Baht currency, I/We allow you to convert the outstanding amount of bill (s) / draft (s) in such other currency into Thai Baht currency by using exchange rate which you deem appropriate and I/We shall pay you default interest on that amount at the rate mentioned above. I/We understand that you may change the default rate without any prior notice to me/us. The calculation of default interest shall commence from the date that I/We default in performance and/or payment up until I/We have paid all obligation to you in full.

I / We agree that the foreign exchange rate be fixed by you using spot on maturity of the relative bill (s) / draft (s) unless otherwise agreed upon.

Should the documents subsequently received appear to have any discrepancy, I/we undertake to take up the documents and authorize you to release the Guarantee/Reserve and pay.

I/We hereby confirm that on the date hereof, I/We have received from you the amount of the bill/draft referred to in the below table and such amount be considered as loan advanced by you to me/us in connection with the trust receipt facility pursuant to the terms hereof.

I / We hereby agree to be jointly & severally liable with the applicant for the fulfilment of the promises and agreements as per this Trust Receipt including extensions renewals and modifications and in the event of default, promise to make good and pay on demand any loss or damage suffered by the **KASIKORNBANK** PUBLIC COMPANY LIMITED Bangkok waiving hereby expressively any defence that may be interposed to any claim or action thereon or here on, especially also as to the order in which the **KASIKORNBANK** PUBLIC COMPANY LIMITED shall choose to reimburse itself.

Guarantor

Yours faithfully,

Authorized Signature

L/C NO.		PARTICULARS OF BILL (S) / DRAFT (S) AND GOODS		
FB NO. (S)				
AMOUNT OF BILL / DRAFT	DUE DATE	DESCRIPTION OF GOODS	MARK(S) AND No. (S)	VESSEL

Prepared by	Checked by		Approved by

9905006-1-09

Source:http://www.kasikornbank.com/EN/ApplyForServices/ApplyForServiceForm/TRU

ST_RECEIPT.pdf

ธนาคารกสิกรไทย
KASIKORNBANK ธนาคารไทย

LETTER OF UNDERTAKING
FOR
ISSUING A LETTER OF GUARANTEE
AND / OR
ENDORSING DELIVERY ORDER

Applicant's Name

Applicant's Address

TO KASIKORNBANK PUBLIC COMPANY LIMITED
HEAD OFFICE 1 SOI KASIKORNTHAI, RATBURANA ROAD, BANGKOK 10140 THAILAND
TEL. +66 2222 0000 FAX +66 2470 1144-5

Date

Dear Sir,

In consideration of your issuing the accompanying Letter of Guarantee and / or endorsing the accompanying Delivery Order for delivery of the under-mentioned goods valued at

(   )

In case the goods have been delivered under the Letter of Guarantee, we, the undersigned Applicant, undertake to hold you free and harmless from any loss or consequences that may arise by such issuing and / or endorsing and we undertake to return to you the said Letter of Guarantee directly as soon as the relative Bill of Lading comes into our possession

In the event that you had to make any payment in pursuant to and / or under your issuing letter of Guarantee and / or endorsing the Delivery Order, we shall fully reimburse you for such your payment

Should the documents subsequently received appear to have any discrepancy, we undertake to take up the documents and your obligations and / or liabilities under such Letter of Guarantee and / or such endorsing Delivery Order shall have been entirely released

Yours faithfully,

DETAILS OF GOODS PER COMMERCIAL INVOICE

Marks and No. (s)	Description of Goods	Vessel	Shippers

Guarantee No.	B/L, A.W.B No.	Checked by	Approved by
	L/C No.		

9902058-1-09

source:http://www.kasikornbank.com/EN/ApplyForServices/ApplyForServiceForm/LETTER_OF_UNDERTAKING_FOR_ISSUING_A_LETTER_OF_GUARANTEE.pdf

1. Goods consigned from (Exporter's name, address, country)	Reference No.
	THE AGREEMENT ON COMPREHENSIVE ECONOMIC PARTNERSHIP AMONG MEMBER STATES OF THE ASSOCIATION OF SOUTHEAST ASIAN NATIONS AND JAPAN (AJCEP AGREEMENT)
2. Goods consigned to (Importer's/consignee's name, address, country)	CERTIFICATE OF ORIGIN FORM AJ
	Issued in Malaysia
	See Notes Overleaf

3. Means of transport and route (as far as known)	4. For official use
Shipment Date	☐ Preferential Treatment Given Under AJCEP Agreement
	☐ Preferential Treatment Not Given (Please state reason/s)
Vessel's Name/Aircraft, etc.	
Port of Discharge	
	Signature of Authorised Signatory of the Importing Country

5. Item number	6. Marks and numbers of packages	7. Number and type of packages, description of goods (including quantity where appropriate and HS number of the importing Party)	8. Origin criteria (see Notes overleaf)	9. Quantity (gross or net weight or other quantity and value, e.g. FOB if required by exporting Party)	10. Number and date of invoices

11. Declaration by the exporter	12. Certification
The undersigned hereby declares that the above details and statements are correct; that all the goods were produced in	It is hereby certified, on the basis of control carried out, that the declaration by the exporter is correct.
.... (Country) and that they comply with the requirements specified for these goods in the AJCEP Agreement for the goods exported to	
.... (Importing Country)	
Place and date, signature and company of Authorised Signatory	Place and date, signature and stamp of Certifying Authority

13. ☐ Third-Country Invoicing   ☐ Back-to-Back CO   ☐ Issued Retroactively

Source:http://www.jadi.com.my/wpcontent/uploads/2010/04/Form-AJ.jpg

1. Goods consigned from (Exporter's business name, address, country)	Reference No.

**ASEAN TRADE IN GOODS AGREEMENT /
ASEAN INDUSTRIAL COOPERATION SCHEME
CERTIFICATE OF ORIGIN**
(Combined Declaration and Certificate)
FORM D

Issued in Singapore

See Overleaf Notes

2. Goods consigned to (Consignee's name, address, country)	

3. Means of transport and route (as far as known) Departure Date Vessel's Name/Aircraft etc. Port of Discharge	4. For Official Use

4. For Official Use

☐ Preferential Treatment Given Under ASEAN Trade in Goods Agreement

☐ Preferential Treatment Given Under ASEAN Industrial Cooperation Scheme

☐ Preferential Treatment Not Given (Please state reason/s)

Signature of Authorised Signatory of the importing Country

5. Item number	6. Marks and numbers on packages	7. Number and type of packages, description of goods (including quantity where appropriate and HS number of the importing country)	8. Origin Criterion (see Overleaf Notes)	9. Gross weight or other quantity and value (FOB)	10. Number and date of Invoices

11. Declaration by the exporter The undersigned hereby declares that the above details and statement are correct; that all the goods were produced in _____ (Country) and that they comply with the origin requirements specified for these goods in the ASEAN Trade in Goods Agreement for the goods exported to _____ (Importing Country) _____ Place and date, signature of authorised signatory	12. Certification It is hereby certified, on the basis of control carried out, that the declaration by the exporter is correct. _____ Place and date, signature and stamp of certifying authority

13.
☐ Third-Country Invoicing ☐ Exhibition
☐ Accumulation ☐ De Minimis
☐ Back-to-Back CO ☐ Issued Retroactively
☐ Partial Cumulation

Certificate of Origin

1. Goods consigned from (Exporter's business name, address, country)	Reference No GENERALISED SYSTEM OF PREFERENCES CERTIFICATE OF ORIGIN (Combined declaration and certificate) FORM A Issued in _____ (country) See Notes overleaf
2. Goods consigned to (Consignee's name, address, country)	
3. Means of transport and route (as far as known)	4. For official use

5. Item number	6. Marks and number of packages	7. Number and kind of packages, description of goods	8. Origin criterion (see Notes overleaf)	9. Gross weight or other quantity	10. Number and date of invoices

11. Certification It is hereby certified, on the basis of control carried out, that the declaration by the exporter is correct. _____ Place and date, signature and stamp of certifying authority	12. Declaration by the exporter The undersigned hereby declares that the above details and statements are correct; that all the goods were produced in _____ (country) and that they comply with the origin requirements specified for those goods in the Generalised System of Preferences for goods exported to _____ (importing country) _____ Place and date, signature of authorized signatory

Source:http://www.mofa.go.jp/policy/economy/gsp/specimen-1.pdf